Mindful Parenting
— for —
Autistic Girls

A Practical Guide to Raising Confident Preteens with Autism Spectrum Disorder, Sensory Challenges, and Anxiety—Navigating Friendship, Periods, and the Teenage Years

Table of Contents

A New Perspective

Chapter 1: Understanding Autism in Girls

- What Does Your Daughter's Autism Really Mean?................14

- Why autism looks different in girls 18

- Why do girls frequently receive late diagnoses? 22

- The unseen problems of masking and the differences between men and women are significant. 26

- Easy Ways to Feel Better About Yourself...............................30

- It is important to her that she eliminate concepts that hinder her progress. 34

Chapter 2: Understanding Autism in Girls

- Tips for Dealing with Stress and Anxiety 41

- What to Do If You Feel Sensitive to Rejection? 45

- Ways to Handle Too Many Sensory Experiences 49

- How can I create a relaxing space that she loves? 53

- Simple Ways to Handle Stress Everyday 57

- How to Teach Your Daughter to Control Herself 61

Chapter 3: Growing Up with Autism

- How to Talk About Your Period and Body Changes Without Being Stuck Up 67

- We aim to make her appreciate her body functionally. 70

- Getting her to like her body in a way that works 74

- How can I help her develop friendships? 78

- Teaching Social Rules That Aren't Written Down.................82

Chapter 4: Communication and Learning

- We support expression through speech and body language.. 89

- I am teaching her how to confidently speak up for herself... 93

- Understand why autistic girls struggle to learn and how to help. 97

- She combines her distinct interests to achieve her goals......101

- She's slowing down at her own pace. 105

Chapter 5: Safety, Sexuality, and Building Connection

- How to Help Her Do It on Her Own 115
- Making It Easy to Understand Consent and Limits 119
- We discuss love, gender, and authenticity. 122
- How to Help Her Do It on Her Own 125
- Making It Easy to Understand Consent and Limits 128
- We discuss love, gender, and authenticity. 131

Conclusion   **135**

Resources   **141**

Free Gift   **144**

This book is for all beautiful girls and young women who see and experience the world in their own unique and amazing ways. People who love and guide you should read it. And may these pages give strength, hope, and understanding to every parent, caretaker, and guide who walks this path with love, patience, and unwavering commitment.

Rebecca Elwin

INTRODUCTION

"It takes a village to raise a child. It takes a child with autism to raise the consciousness of the village." – Coach Elaine Hall

A New Perspective

We are different because we are parents, friends, and fans of autism girls. People with autism, like our daughters, sisters, and friends, have situations that don't always fit into popular stories or expectations. This book is both a guide and a source of comfort that the trip you're on has profound meaning and beauty.

We'll discuss problems, solutions, and ways to deal with difficulties in these parts. We will discuss topics that offer useful information and warm support. This is whether you're here to learn more about autism or because you're having trouble with parenting issues. Let's go on this trip with our hearts and minds open.

There are times when you feel happy, scared, and like you're growing up as a parent. But when you have an autistic girl, you may face extra problems and questions that make you feel alone and confused. There are many tools out there today that are mostly about boys or talk about autism in a way that doesn't show how girls' experiences are different.

In order to fill that gap, this book, Parenting Autistic Girls: A Practical Guide to Raising Confident Preteens with Autism Spectrum Disorder, Sensory Challenges, and Anxiety, was written. This is meant to give you, as a parent, teacher, or guide, ideas and methods that will help autistic girls grow, learn, and become the amazing people they were meant to be.

Why was this book written?

Autism spectrum disorder (ASD) is more common in boys than in girls, which means girls with ASD have fewer resources. Their symptoms and experiences can be very different from boys'. Part of the reason for this difference is that most autism studies have been done on male habits and traits. So, many autistic girls have been given the wrong diagnosis or too late, often after years of not knowing or feeling like they belong. This book is meant to fill that gap, offer personalized help, and recognize autistic girls' special journey.

Getting ready for special autism problems

One big difference between autism girls and other girls is how they handle social settings. Their ability to "mask," or hide symptoms so they can fit in with their peers, is often better. This ability to change may help them avoid being rejected immediately, but it often costs them emotionally. Masking can make worries more pronounced, lower self-esteem, or even delay a diagnosis. Parents and other adults who care for girls may see them "keeping it together" at school or in social situations, but when they get home, they may be tired, stressed out, or having an emotional meltdown. People whose girls are struggling with this may not know how to help them. This book gives girls useful tips on how to accept themselves as they are and feel confident without hiding who they are.

Help with emotions and useful strategies

This book is written with you, the parent or caretaker, in mind for every part. We will discuss how autism affects girls in particular and the problems of being a teenage autistic. But it's not just about the problems; you also want to help your daughter find happiness, confidence, and freedom on her own terms. This book gives useful tips for everyday situations, like how to deal with physical issues, make friends, and understand how your body changes.

For instance, when you look up "sensory sensitivities," you'll find tools and suggestions that will enable you to make calm and comfortable places for your daughter. You will also learn relaxation techniques to help her deal with stressful situations. These skills will enable her to feel better emotionally now and in the future.

There are five main parts to the book, and each talks about a different time or part of raising a girl with autism.

Part 1: How to Understand Autism in Girls First, we discuss what autism means for girls, busting some popular myths along the way, and why girls are more likely to be diagnosed later than boys. Self-esteem plays a big part in this section, and parents can help their girls let go of negative ideas that hold them back.

Part 2: Dealing with Feelings and Sensory Issues Girls on the autism spectrum may have trouble with their senses and strong feelings, which can be too much for some. We'll discuss ways to deal with these big feelings, tools for making spaces more relaxing, and ways to promote awareness and self-regulation in this part.

Part 3: Having Autism as a Child Physical and mental changes happen during puberty, and it can be especially problematic for girls with autism. This part talks about how to talk about sensitive topics like body changes. It also talks about building positive body image and dealing with friendship complications.

Part 4: Communicating and Learning—Many autistic girls have trouble communicating both verbally and nonverbally, which can make school and relationships challenging for them. You can use the ideas in this article to help your daughter express herself and learn useful skills that will help her become independent.

Part 5: Getting Safe, Being Sexual, and Making Friends In the last part, we discuss key safety issues, setting limits, and making connections that matter. This part talks about peer pressure, finding organizations that support and encourage her, and figuring out who she is.

This book is about working together, both with your daughter and with other parents and with autism patients in general. We can ensure that girls on the range feel accepted, understood, and capable by learning about their unique strengths and problems. This book wants to be your guide on this journey by giving you tools, ideas, and comfort along the way.

How to Read and Use This Book

You could read this book from beginning to end or skip to the parts that are most helpful for you right now. There are tasks, real-life examples, and ideas in each chapter that you can use right away. Never forget that each child with autism is unique and that there is no one "appropriate" way to parent. You can find help in this book, but work with your gut and change the suggestions to fit your daughter's wants and personality.

Taking Steps Forward with Faith

Taking care of an autism girl is a journey of love, strength, and learning. Some days will be a challenge to handle because of strong feelings and problems that seem impossible to solve. However, there will also be beautiful, growing, and joyous times. Your daughter is starting a unique journey. With your help, she can become a strong, self-assured young woman who knows her worth and loves her strengths.

Let's go down this road together. There are many stages in a girl's life, from teenager to young adult. This book will help you and your daughter through them all.

Chapter 1: Understanding Autism in Girls

"Autism is not a puzzle, nor a disease. Autism is a challenge, but certainly not a devastating one." – Trisha Van Berkel

What Does Your Daughter's Autism Really Mean?

People often see eye contact as a sign of interest, friendliness, and desire to connect. It feels normal to many people. However, making eye contact can be an unusual experience for autism girls. If your daughter avoids eye contact, it's not because she's rude or doesn't care. It's because striking eye contact with her might be too much for her or even cause her nervous. Think about looking straight at the sun. For some autistic girls, maintaining eye contact can be challenging, making it difficult to act in this manner.

This doesn't mean she's not paying attention or wanting to connect with others. Girls with autism often pay close attention to talks and pick up on details that others might miss, even if they are glanced at something else. However, in our culture, maintaining eye contact is crucial as it signifies honesty and interest. Because of this mistake, her teachers, friends, and even family may get the wrong idea of her behavior. They may think she's not involved or telling the truth when she's just processing things in her own way.

In one situation, your daughter might be at a family get-together and sit quietly while the adults talk. She's not looking at anyone in particular. She's looking at her hands, playing with her ring, and maybe even scanning around the room. As someone unfamiliar with autism, you may believe that she isn't paying attention to what is being said. However, it's possible that she is actively listening and absorbing everything. Her interaction style isn't necessarily different; it's simply different.

Researchers have found that making autistic people make eye contact doesn't always help them interact with others better. Temple Grandin, a well-known advocate for autistic people, once said, "I tend to stare in someone's general direction rather than directly at them." "This way it is easier to listen to." Parents can feel so much better when they understand this. For her own safety, you don't need to "train" her to look people in the eye. Tell her that listening to what she wants is fine—there's no "right" or "wrong" way.

Autism lacks a distinct appearance.

When people think about autism, one of the biggest myths is that there is a "look"—a set of obvious signs that someone is autistic. This belief is not only false, but it can also cause significant harm as it leads people to ignore or reject autistic girls. This is true even if they don't exhibit the typical "look" associated with autism. Autism is a brain difference, not a disease. There is no single facial expression, body language, or behavior that consistently indicates autism.

Your daughter is probably just another kid when she's out in public, like on the field, at school, or with friends. She might not act in ways most people consider autism-related. This can cause people to not understand or care about her problems. People might say things like, "She doesn't seem abnormal" or "She looks normal to me," which could make her feel like her problems aren't real.

Imagine the following scenario: a group of adults are at a playground. They're talking about their kids, and one mom brings up her daughter has autism. When one parent looks over and sees a happy, active girl, they ask, "Really?" Someone said, "She doesn't appear disabled." This may seem like an innocent comment, but it has a significant impact. These comments suggest that autism requires visible manifestation. This means that autistic girls feel like they have to show they are autistic to get their needs met. This kind of confusion is tiring and can make autistic girls feel excluded.

In real life, autism is difficult to observe. You must listen and accept what an autistic person says to understand their struggles. Autism really doesn't have a "look"; it has a voice, a point of view, and a special way of being in the world. Acknowledging this leads to the dismantling of preconceived notions and facilitates a broader, more empathetic understanding of autism.

For autistic girls, feelings can be challenging to understand. Society usually expects girls to be emotional and caring, but autistic girls may show their feelings in different ways, which can cause confusion. Some girls with autism may seem cold or uninterested, even when they're really feeling something.

Some people may overreact to minor issues. This unique way of feeling and showing emotions doesn't mean they don't have empathy or emotional depth; it just means they show it in ways that others might not notice.

Think about a day when your daughter just got home from school. Despite her apparent anger, she remains silent when you inquire about her day. She might shut herself off in her room to get some peace and quiet. As a parent, it's normal to feel scared or disappointed when this happens. Your partner might even make you wonder if something is wrong. But most of the time, her silence is just a way to deal with her feelings and take care of herself. This is not because she doesn't like you. This is one way autistic girls calm down, especially after something stressful.

Many times, people misinterpret these moments and assume the person isn't experiencing emotions. Studies, on the other hand, show that autistic people, including girls, often feel very strongly about things; they just have different ways of showing or dealing with these feelings.

Autism expert psychologist Dr. Tony Attwood says, "Autistic people experience strong emotions." The problem is communication, not how people react.

Rather than pressuring her to behave normally, it can be beneficial to help her comprehend her emotions. You could recommend that when she feels overwhelmed, she draws or writes in a notebook. For her, these kinds of activities work better than normal talks. This is because they let her be herself without feeling like she has to fit in with what others expect of her.

<u>Change and Introspection</u>

The more you learn about these small but profound changes in how your daughter deals with the world, the better you can help her. With all of its subtleties, difficulties, and beauty, autism in girls doesn't fit easily into a single description or stereotype. It's an exciting and complicated experience that needs understanding, openness, and readiness to let go of assumptions.

Consider your daughter's self-talk and perception. How can you change your mind when you see her avoiding eye contact, looking "normal," or acting differently when upset? What can you do to accept her unique interactions with the world? How might knowing these small details help her feel more accepted and strong in a world that might not always get her?.

WHY AUTISM LOOKS DIFFERENT IN GIRLS

What does social conditioning do to hide autism traits?

From a young age, people often tell girls to be caring, helpful, and emotionally aware of others, sometimes openly and sometimes quietly. Society has different standards for girls than for boys, and autistic girls feel this just as much as other girls. Girls with autism often hide their autism by copying social cues others use, whether they know it or not. Masking is a vital skill for many girls on the spectrum because it helps them fit in with their peers without standing out too much.

Picture a little girl at school who tries desperately to be like her friends. She notices how they make eye contact and laugh and keeps track of the small smiles and nods during their talks. She needs to practice and improve her skills at this social dance, as it is not something she naturally excels at. She might get so proficient at this over time that not even her closest friends will know she's hiding. Behind the scenes, it's tedious work. She may experience mental exhaustion every day when returning home from work due to the constant pressure to appear neurotypical.

Masking is a strong idea because it helps autistic girls get along in a world that doesn't always understand them. However, it also leads to significant conflict within the group. Imagine how this affects her self-worth, leading her to believe that her true self is wrong or unworthy simply because it doesn't align with societal expectations. Girls with autism who always wear masks may lose touch with themselves. This can add to their anxiety and nervousness, which lasts into adulthood.

Due to their social training, autism girls tend to be more self-centered. Some boys might act out their problems by having temper tantrums, but girls take it out on themselves instead, which can cause worry, sadness, or self-doubt. An important autism researcher, Dr. Tony Attwood, said, "Autistic girls are the great camouflage experts of the human world." Understanding how social conditioning affects autistic girls helps us understand why they might hide their traits and how important it is to help them feel safe enough to be themselves.

How Hormone Differences Affect Girls' Autism Awareness

A significant part of understanding why autism shows up differently in girls is that their hormones are different. When it comes to controlling emotions, sensitivities, and even social behavior, hormones, especially those related to puberty, play a big role. As girls approach puberty, estrogen levels can accentuate autism symptoms while masking others. For example, many parents notice that their child's emotional and sensory sensitivity gets increasingly severe during puberty. This can cause them to have stronger reactions to sounds, smells, or even social situations that they used to find acceptable.

Imagine that your daughter is transitioning from a kid to an adolescent. She may feel different emotions or have new physical issues. She might no longer tolerate certain clothes due to extreme itching. Because of noise or lights, a room that used to feel cozy may now seem too big. Her hormones closely correlate with these changes, further complicating her autism.

Hormonal changes also affect how people act around others. One example is that when estrogen levels rise, it can make girls with autism even more aware of social cues and interactions. This increased awareness can make her want to connect with others even more. However, it may also show her how different her experiences are from those of her peers, leading her to feel a lot more alone or different. But these changes in her hormones may make it harder to hide than before. What seemed doable before might be too much for her now, and she might need more space to get back on track.

Hormones can affect mental health. Studies show that autistic girls are more likely to experience anxiety and sadness, especially during adolescence. This is partly because of how hormonal changes and social factors affect girls at this age.

Parents can feel better when they understand this link. It helps them see that their child's actions are not signs of resistance or "moodiness," but rather a real need for help during a physically and mentally rough time.

Why the usual autism diagnosis might miss girls with autism

For a long time, boys' studies have formed the foundation of autism diagnostic standards. This has led to the omission or incorrect diagnosis of many autistic girls. Since the beginning of the autism study, it has focused mostly on behaviors more common in boys. These behaviors include being hyperactive or not interested in certain things. This implies that we often overlook the subtle symptoms of autistic girls. This gap in diagnosis sometimes prevents girls who don't fit the "classic" autism description from receiving the necessary help.

Think of it as a diagnosis checklist. It might be about repetitive behaviors, intense hobbies, or interpersonal relationships. A boy with autism might show these traits in more obvious ways, while a girl with autism might do so in more subtle ways. Instead of having a strong interest in trains or numbers, a girl with autism may have a "special interest," such as collecting toys or repeatedly reading a specific set of books. They might seem normal at first glance, so teachers, doctors, or even parents are less likely to notice anything strange about them.

The old ways of diagnosing autism also miss the fact that autistic girls often struggle inside. Some boys may have problems that are readily apparent to see, like sensory overload or social cues, but many girls hide them. They might struggle through tough times in silence because they don't want to stand out or let others down. This behavior doesn't lessen autism; it simply manifests itself in a distinct manner. As a result, many autistic girls remain undiagnosed until they reach their teens or even adulthood, leaving them to ponder why they feel "different."

Delays in detection can cause numerous additional problems. Identifying girls later in life may lead them to believe for years that they are "defective" or not attractive enough. They might have attributed their problems to personality flaws rather than brain differences. Consider the impact on their mental health and self-esteem if they experienced confusion or a sense of being "not quite right" for years due to autism's unexpected nature.

Researchers like Dr. Judith Gould, a clinical psychologist who specializes in autism in girls, are pushing for more open diagnosing standards, which is a step in the right direction. Dr. Gould asserts that autism manifests itself in a variety of ways, many of which conventional diagnosis methods still struggle to fully comprehend. Realizing this makes it possible to find autistic girls earlier and give them and their families the help they need.

<u>Change and Introspection</u>

It's simple to understand why diagnosing and helping girls with autism can be challenging: social training, hormonal differences, and the fact that diagnostic standards aren't always accurate. This intricate understanding is crucial as it enables you to comprehend the potential misinterpretation, disregard, or incorrect diagnosis of your daughter.

Consider the impact of your daughter's social training on her daily life. Have you noticed that her behavior has changed as her hormones change? Additionally, do you believe that the diagnosis process has significantly impacted her experience? These questions can help you achieve your highest level of helpfulness and understanding.

WHY DO GIRLS FREQUENTLY RECEIVE LATE DIAGNOSES?

When people mistake autism for anxiety or ADHD due to overlapping symptoms

When we think of autism, we often think of very specific habits. These habits include having trouble with social relationships, doing the same things over and over, and being very interested in certain things. Autism can look very different in girls, though. In fact, many girls exhibit symptoms similar to other conditions, such as nervousness or ADHD. This can lead professionals and even parents to misinterpret these signs. Instead of seeing autism, they might believe the child has attention deficit problems, missing the deeper, more complicated truth.

Recall a time when your daughter was in school, displaying signs of nervousness in groups, frequently fidgeting, or requiring additional assistance to maintain focus. People may label her as a "worrier" or suggest that she struggles with attention, yet these behaviors stem from common physical sensitivity or social discomfort among autism patients. However, due to the typical association of anxiety and ADHD with behaviors such as excessive worry or difficulty concentrating, autism, which lies at the core of her experience, may remain hidden. Many girls feel confused and have difficulty meeting social standards for years without knowing why.

Professionals, even well-meaning ones, can miss autism signs in girls. This is because they are too focused on "classic" signs of ADHD or nervousness. Girls may seek therapy to manage their nervousness, yet these methods fail to fully address autism's underlying issue. Consider how exhausting it must be for a girl to attend classes designed to "relax" her anxiety, given that it stems from events she encounters due to her autism. It's like taking medication for cold symptoms without addressing the underlying cause.

So many people mix autism with other diagnoses that experts are now stressing how critical it is for doctors to look deeper than just the signs. Dr. Samantha Laugeson, a clinical psychologist specializing in autism, emphasizes the importance of delving deeper into the primary causes of these behaviors. This is rather than focusing solely on their outward appearance. This can be life-changing for girls who have struggled with a diagnosis that doesn't quite fit. If girls know these signs, they can get the right help and understand and love their true selves without constantly worrying about misinterpretation.

What does gender bias do to autism research and diagnosis?

Gender bias isn't just a term in everyday life; it happens in autism research and diagnosis. Most studies on autism in the past focused on boys, and the diagnosis criteria relied on actions common to autism boys. The autism study used what we call "the male prototype" for many years. This meant that traits common in boys were considered normal signs of autism, while traits prevalent in girls remained unnoticed. This means that girls with autism often don't fit this standard mold, leading experts to overlook their autism.

Imagine a medical tool based on boys' actions. It could focus on stereotypical interests like trains, numbers, or technical things. It could also focus on behaviors that are simple to see and do over and over again. On the other hand, a girl with autism may exhibit interests typical of her age and gender. For example, a strong interest in animals or sharing stories. These interests don't appear unusual, reducing the likelihood of raising concerns. These interests could captivate her just as much as boys. Due to this subtle distinction, girls with autism often do not receive the support a label could provide. They have to carry their condition alone.

Stereotypes based on gender also influence how people perceive girls with psychological problems. While boys on the autism spectrum may struggle with social norms, many girls mimic them. We refer to this as "social camouflage," where girls mimic their peers' actions or words to blend in. But this camouflage comes at a high emotional cost, often leading to anxiety or burnout. Diagnostic standards fail to consider this skill of masking, resulting in the missed diagnosis of many girls whose autism remains hidden behind their carefully constructed, societally acceptable façade.

This tendency has substantial implications. Unidentified girls often face the consequences on their own, believing they are simply "different" without understanding why. Dr. Judith Gould, one of the first people to study autism, said, "The diagnostic criteria were developed based on how boys show autism, which doesn't represent the experiences of many girls." It is important to be aware of this gender bias in diagnostic standards so that autistic girls can get the support and validation they need. They struggle to fit into social norms that never make sense for them without this support.

Schools and parents often miss the first signs of autism.

A lot of girls meet people other than their family for the first time at school. Parents and teachers both have a big part to play in noticing and pointing out differences in how kids grow. However, due to the subtle nature of autism in girls, individuals lacking training may miss early signs. Teachers and parents may mistakenly attribute a child's behavior to personality traits or shyness, oblivious to the fact that these behaviors are actually signs of autism.

Imagine that your daughter sits quietly in a busy classroom and never talks. Because of sense issues, she might find it challenging to follow spoken directions or stay away from group activities. A teacher might think that her behavior is just a sign that she is shy or quiet, which are normal traits for girls her age. On the inside, she might be feeling too much because she is trying to handle sensory information and social cues at the same time. This feels too much. People tend to overlook her problems because she avoids drawing attention to herself. In fact, they might even praise her for her "appropriate behavior."

Similarly, parents may overlook these signs at home, especially if their daughter appears to be performing well at school or with friends. Girls may hold their stress inside, while boys may act out by having temper tantrums or being too focused on certain things. They might pull away from people and only want to be with a small group of close friends or do things alone at home. Parents may think, "She's just independent," not understanding that her desire for silence is a way for her to deal with the pressures of being around many people.

It can be challenging for both teachers and parents to comprehend that autism encompasses more than just social difficulties or unusual hobbies. It involves how your daughter perceives, thinks, and feels about the world. Boys on the spectrum may show these traits more readily, but girls on the spectrum often learn to fit in, which makes it more difficult to see the problems they face. Early detection of these minor signs can make all the difference in getting her the help she needs to grow in a way that respects her true self.

Dr. Sarah Cassidy, an expert on autism and gender differences, stated that autistic girls often remain unnoticed. Their presence is invisible unless you know how they appear. Teachers and parents who know this can be more thoughtful about early observations and give their daughter support that fits her needs. This is instead of pushing her to fit in with what others expect.

<u>Change and Introspection</u>

When you think about how autism can be confused for other conditions, how gender bias affects people, and the small signs that teachers and parents often miss, you start to understand why so many autistic girls are diagnosed later in life. Knowing these issues is the first step to making your daughter feel seen and encouraged.

Think about what your daughter has been through. Have people ever called her actions "anxious" or "distracted"? Does it bother you that the conventional understanding of autism may not have met her needs? How might this information help you speak up for her better in the future?

Now that you know these things, let's discuss the next topic: "The Hidden Challenges of Masking and Gender Differences."

THE UNSEEN PROBLEMS OF MASKING AND THE DIFFERENCES BETWEEN MEN AND WOMEN ARE SIGNIFICANT.

How do you mask, and why do girls do it?

Imagine seeing a play where the lead character has to change their lines, tone, and facial reactions all the time. This is to match what everyone else on stage is doing. The character is so focused on fitting in that she cannot fully enjoy the experience. For many autistic girls, covering is like putting on a show all the time to "fit in" and look like everyone else. Girls with autism get through social settings by masking, which means copying their peers' actions, gestures, and speech habits. While men may display autistic traits, women conceal them.

When they are young, girls with ASD may notice that their natural reactions differ from others'. They might notice that some jokes make their friends laugh or that they talk in a certain way. Instead of letting their real emotions show, they copy these cues and try to fit in. Most people don't intentionally hide who they are—it's a survival strategy to prevent ridicule, misinterpretation, or rejection. Many people engage in this practice so frequently that it resembles putting on an outfit every morning before venturing out into the world.

It costs something to hide, though. Throughout every setting, girls must remain mentally and physically alert in order to monitor their behavior, conceal certain traits, and adhere to social norms. Consider a schoolgirl who, despite not fully understanding what others say, mimics their laughter and nods. This is what she knows will make her seem more "normal," but on the inside, she may feel detached, lonely, and worn out. Girls can avoid immediate social problems by masking, but it also forces them to choose between authenticity and acceptance.

Autism expert Dr. Tony Attwood says that covering is like a "chameleon effect," where autistic girls change to fit in with their surroundings to avoid unwanted attention. But this change often makes things difficult in the long run, even though it works in the short term. If parents and other adults who care for autistic girls understand why these girls frequently remove their masks and express themselves without fear of judgment, they can create a safe environment for them to do so.

How masking hurts mental health and self-esteem

Masking costs money, especially for a girl's mental health and sense of who she is. Girls who mask deny aspects of their true selves to conform to social norms. In the long run, this can make her feel cut off from who she really is, like the "mask" she's wearing has a life of its own. This tension inside her between who she really is and who she thinks she should be can make her feel anxious, depressed, and like she doesn't have any worth.

Imagine how heavy it is on your emotions to always hide parts of yourself because you think, feel, and want things that aren't "good enough." It's akin to carrying a hidden burden that intensifies over time. Autistic girls mask daily. Because it's so natural for them, they might not even know they're doing it. But the emotional toll adds up, and many people experience what they call "autistic burnout"—a state of mental and physical tiredness from avoiding it for a long time.

When the pressure to hide intensifies, such as during youth or adulthood, burnout often manifests. As people get older, their goals and social relationships get more complicated. Girls with autism may wonder who they are and ask, "Who am I if I'm always pretending to be someone else?" Identity crises can be very painful because they may not know who they are or who they've been trying to be.

Mental health is affected. Research has shown that autistic girls who mask are more likely to have anxiety, sadness, and even suicidal ideas. Masking keeps them from connecting with others, but also with themselves. Dr. Sarah Cassidy, an expert on autism, states that pretending ensnares the individual in an invisible cage, where they are forced to be someone they are not. It's critical for their mental health to find places to take off their masks. The first step toward helping them find peace with their true selves is seeing and dealing with hiding effects.

Gender norms and how they affect autism patients

Our society has deeply ingrained standards for girls and boys, which significantly influence autism manifestation and perception. From a young age, we teach girls to be caring, polite, and socially aware. These expectations can clash with autism traits, making autistic girls feel even more pressure to hide their differences and "fit in." While boys might accept being "quirky" or "a bit of a loner," the expectation for girls to be adept at interacting with others often hinders autistic girls from expressing their true desires.

Imagine a school where girls receive praise for playing with others and making friends, while boys receive advice to concentrate on their own goals. This kind of social pressure can be too much for an autistic girl. She might perceive expectations that don't align with her inherent preferences. For example, she may enjoy doing things by herself or be very interested in a certain subject. She learns to hide her interests and smile and nods, even though she doesn't fully understand how to connect with others. Gender norms make it easier for autistic girls to stay out of trouble, as they tend to act like everyone else, hiding their true selves.

These standards may lead autistic girls to perceive their social problems as a personal flaw rather than a normal difference. This is even when they are experiencing difficulties. They might not think, "I'm different, and that's okay," but rather, "There's something wrong with me." This feeling of not being satisfactory enough, stemming from social standards, can lead to negative self-image and low self-esteem. Society sends girls subtle but constant messages about how they "should" act, which makes autistic girls feel like they have to fit in instead of being themselves.

A well-known person who supports disabled people once said, "The world needs all kinds of minds." These words tell us that our society benefits from variety, and that includes neurological diversity. However, gender norms can hinder autistic girls from utilizing their unique skills, just as they hinder boys from doing so. As parents and other adults who care for girls, be aware of these standards and provide space to escape them. You can convey a powerful message to your girl that she doesn't need to conform to all societal norms to gain acceptance and respect.

<u>Change and Introspection</u>

Knowing about covering, how it affects the mind, and how gender norms play a role helps us see the hidden problems autistic girls face. Think about these questions: Does your daughter change how she acts when with others? Have you seen signs of being tired or frustrated trying to "fit in"? Additionally, could gender norms influence her approach to autism?

Let's move on to the next part of this trip and discuss ways to boost her confidence. This will enable her to be herself without hiding behind a mask.

Easy Ways to Feel Better About Yourself

There are different skills and hobbies for each child. Autistic girls have highly specific and profound interests. Society often tells girls they need to fit into certain molds. But your daughter will be most confident when she accepts her unique skills and interests. Supporting her hobbies, whether animals, art, or space, can help her feel positive about herself. When she knows others appreciate her interests, she feels secure enough to explore and share them. This lets her true personality shine.

Remember the moments when your daughter gets incredibly excited about something she loves? Maybe she's really into a certain kind of music and can remember the words to songs very well, or maybe she loves building with Legos and constructing structures you'd never think of. Celebrate her skills with her. Let her know that the talents she has are very valuable and useful. Don't try to lead her toward what her friends think is "popular" or "cool." Instead, show her that her own hobbies are of importance. She will understand that she doesn't have to change to fit in—what makes her unique is what makes her strong.

As an example of real life, I worked with a family whose daughter was very interested in marine biology. She knew everything about sea species, from the smallest jellyfish to the biggest whales, even though she was very young. She was able to do this because her parents took her to aquariums, let her lead conversations with marine scientists, and helped her give short talks at school. This not only helped her learn, but also made her feel better about herself. Her parents praised her special interests, which made her feel smart and valuable.

You must allow her the freedom to explore her hobbies without fear of judgment to support her uniqueness. Girls with autism are often very focused and interested in one thing. See this as a source of strength instead of a passion or a thing that holds you back. "The world needs all kinds of minds," famously said Temple Grandin, a prominent supporter of autistic people. Letting your daughter follow her interests shows her that she is welcome in the world, even though she has a "different" mind.

Celebrating small wins can build confidence.

You don't get more confident overnight. Learn to trust yourself and appreciate your small successes. Celebrating the small wins, like getting along with someone, mastering an additional skill, or just facing a tough situation with grace, helps her see her strengths and make progress in her life. You don't have to be a perfectionist; you just have to work hard and grow. Every step forward is significant to her, so she values her path, even if it doesn't look like anyone else's.

Your daughter might have a challenging time in groups, but one day she can handle a short group task at school without getting too stressed out. Good job. She might also consider trying something challenging, such as giving a brief speech, despite her fear of public speaking. That's another win. Have fun with her during these times. Let her know that you see how hard she's working and how far she's come. This is more critical than any result. It's not necessary to do something big to celebrate. A simple "I saw how brave you were today" or "I'm proud of you for trying something that felt hard" can mean a lot.

A mom I know told me she always celebrated her daughter's wins, no matter how small. She had trouble making eye contact with her daughter at first, but with gentle guidance, she learned to do it with family members over time. Every time she did it, her mom praised her without pressure, which made her feel proud of her bravery and dedication to work. Over time, this built trust and confidence. Her daughter felt safe in her success because her family saw how much she worked.

Remember that confidence grows over time, and these small victories add up to a bigger self-assurance. When your daughter sees herself successful, even in small ways, she stops talking badly about herself. It tells them, "I can do this." She learns to be proud of her progress, which makes her stronger and more ready to face obstacles, sure she can handle them one step at a time.

We teach kids how to talk to themselves positively and be strong.

How we talk to ourselves can change how we feel about ourselves. Learning positive self-talk is very beneficial for autistic girls who may have problems with self-doubt or feel like they are "not like others." You can give her the strength to deal with problems and failures by encouraging her to find a positive inner voice. Show her that cultivating self-kindness is a skill she can master, transforming it into a lifelong source of power.

You can start by telling yourself positive things or reminding yourself of them. For example, if she's nervous about going to a social event, encourage her, "It's okay to be myself" or "I am strong and capable." These simple phrases may seem insignificant, but if she says them to herself often, they can change her attitude and help her feel safe in social situations. Tell her to think of nicer things instead of negative ones. She could say, "I'm learning, and each time I do it better," instead of, "I'm not skilled at this."

A girl I worked with used to get really nervous before speaking in front of her class. Her mother told her to engage in positive self-talk, like telling herself, "I have enlightened things to say" and "I can do this." Over time, her nervousness went away, and she felt more ready to face similar problems. She said these mantras over and over again until they became normal parts of her mind. This gave her the confidence to face things that used to scare her.

Another important skill that will help her throughout her life is resilience. Things can go wrong in life, and building her grit will help her deal with problems with confidence and flexibility. This doesn't mean avoiding problems; it means learning how to get back up after they happen. When things get tough, you can help her become more resilient by recognizing her feelings and helping her find answers or new ways to look at things. For instance, if she has a failure or setback, like not being able to make friends in a new class, tell her to focus on what she can control, like finding things she has in common with her peers, instead of dwelling on what didn't go as planned.

"Effort is a path to mastery," said Dr. Carol Dweck, a psychologist known for her work on mindset. Teaching her to value her efforts, not just the results, makes her quite strong. She will learn that it's not important to be perfect, but to try, learn, and be sure that she can handle anything that comes her way. She's learning the skills she needs to handle the ups and downs of life with courage and a sense of self-worth by talking positively to herself and being strong.

<u>Change and Introspection</u>

As you support her unique skills, enjoy her victories, and help her stay strong, you're building a strong sense of self-worth that comes from being true to herself. Think about how these ways can help her on her path. Have you seen her shine in her own special way? What small victories can you celebrate today? And what might changing the way she talks to herself mean for her confidence as she grows?

Let's look at how imperative it is to "Let Go of Stereotypes That Hold Her Back" with these tools in mind.

IT IS IMPORTANT TO HER THAT SHE ELIMINATE CONCEPTS THAT HINDER HER PROGRESS.

We should view autism as a strength rather than a weakness.

People often think of autism in terms of problems and restrictions when discussing it. But what if we changed our minds and saw autism for the special strengths it can bring? The concept of autism as a strength instead of a weakness doesn't mean you don't see the problems. Focus, creativity, and a strong sense of loyalty are some of the admirable traits associated with autism. Your daughter's autism makes her strengths even stronger. Helping her see these strengths as assets can help her accept herself as she is.

Think about how she might be effective at things that others find problematic. She might notice things that other people miss because she has a keen eye for detail, or she might be very interested in something that makes her want to learn more about it in depth. These qualities are crucial and can benefit her at school, with friends, and later in her job. By pointing out these positive things about her, you can let her see that she has something valuable to offer the world.

One parent I knew helped her daughter think about her autism in a new way by highlighting all the positive ways her unique traits assisted others. When her daughter's friends had trouble focusing in class, she told her she was lucky to be able to do so. When her daughter remembered the smallest things about her friends' lives, she told her that this was a sign of empathy. This was even though her daughter had trouble with other social cues. Slowly, her daughter learned to see herself not as "different" in a negative way but as unique and positive in a way that made her stand out.

Dr. Temple Grandin, a well-known autism advocate, said, "Different, not less."

This simple phrase says a lot: being unique doesn't mean being less. Your daughter's autism might make her different from her peers, but it also makes her specially equipped to view the world in ways others might not. She can learn to see her differences as strengths as she grows up. This will help her feel positive about herself and be strong in a world that might not always understand her.

Breaking Free from Men and Women's Acting

Girls have always had to meet certain expectations set by society. These expectations include being caring, adept at making friends, and able to show how they feel. Gender expectations can be particularly challenging for autistic girls, who naturally engage with the world differently. If your daughter doesn't fit these societal expectations, it's imperative to let her know this is okay. Getting rid of these strict standards can be very freeing for her, letting her focus on being herself instead of an image she feels she has to live up to.

Consider the subtle and not-so-subtle messages girls receive: to be "right," they must be considerate, follow rules, and get along... These expectations can be challenging to live up to, especially for a girl with autism who might not normally follow social rules in this way. If she would rather be alone than with others or finds big groups stressful, she may feel like she has to go against her inherent tendencies to "fit in." This can make her feel like her natural behaviors are somehow wrong or unacceptable.

One family faced difficulties when well-meaning relatives encouraged their naturally reserved daughter to become more outgoing at family gatherings. They would tell her to "smile more" or "talk to everyone," not understanding that these interactions felt overwhelming to her. When her parents finally stepped in and told her she didn't have to meet these expectations—that it was okay to be herself—she visibly relaxed. She began to approach gatherings in her own way, comfortable knowing that her parents accepted her just as she was.

Gender expectations can make autistic girls feel like they're failing at "being a girl" if they don't meet society's narrow criteria. But what if we taught our daughters that they're free to define what it means to be a girl on their terms? By breaking down these gendered expectations, we're giving them permission to be their authentic selves. Malala Yousafzai, a renowned advocate for girls' rights, once stated, "We recognize the significance of our voices only when we experience silence." Let's make sure that society's expectations of how our daughters "should" behave never cause them to feel silenced and instead give them the freedom to flourish in ways that respect their uniqueness.

Helping Her Define Success on Her Own Terms

Traditional markers of success don't always align with autistic experience. While society often measures success by external achievements—good grades, a wide social circle, or certain career paths—your daughter might have her own definition of success. Helping her define success on her own terms can free her from comparisons and pressures that don't serve her well. Instead of focusing on fitting into predefined molds, she can explore what makes her feel fulfilled and happy.

Let's imagine your daughter is less interested in having a large group of friends but finds immense joy in one or two deep, meaningful friendships. To her, success might look like connecting deeply with those select friends rather than trying to meet society's expectations of a wide social circle. Or perhaps she's not focused on traditional academic achievements but excels in creative or technical pursuits, like art or coding. In this case, success isn't about grades or standardized tests; it's about cultivating her passions and finding joy in the activities she loves.

One family I know faced this challenge when their daughter, who had a keen interest in animals, struggled academically. Instead of pushing her to excel in areas that didn't resonate with her, they encouraged her to volunteer at a local animal shelter. Through this experience, she got a sense of purpose, and her self-esteem grew because she succeeded in her own way. Rather than measuring herself by academic standards, she found fulfillment in an area that mattered to her.

Encourage your daughter to think about what success feels like to her rather than what it looks like to others. This process might involve exploring her values and interests to understand what brings her satisfaction and joy. "Authenticity is the daily practice of letting go of who we think we should be and embracing who we are," writes Brené Brown. Supporting your daughter in defining success authentically can help her feel empowered to pursue her own path. This is no matter how different it may look from the norm.

<u>Change and Introspection</u>

By helping her reframe autism as a strength, encouraging her to break free from gender expectations, and supporting her in defining success on her own terms, you're giving her the tools to embrace her unique identity fully. Think about how these shifts might impact her life: How can you help her recognize her strengths more openly? Are there gendered expectations she's struggling to meet? And what does success truly mean to her?

With these empowering perspectives, let's explore strategies for "How to Handle Anxiety and Emotional Overwhelm."

Chapter 2: Managing Emotions and Sensory Challenges

"Emotions are like waves. We can't stop them from coming, but we can choose which ones to surf." – Jonatan Mårtensson

Tips for Dealing with Stress and Anxiety

Identifying triggers before they worsen

Worry and stress are not spontaneous feelings. Certain things, which vary greatly for each individual, often trigger these feelings. Understanding the factors that trigger your daughter's anxiety can help her manage it before it escalates. The key thing is to help her figure out what makes her feel that way. This is so she can deal with her feelings confidently. Determining these triggers is not always straightforward; it requires patience, attentiveness, and occasionally investigative work. However, once she grasps the broader perspective, she can regain control over situations that previously left her feeling powerless.

In a normal situation, your daughter feels nervous when she has to step into a place that is large and noisy, like a mall. She begins to feel more and more panicked as her breathing speeds up and her hands move around. Knowing that her nervousness usually gets more intense in busy places will help her get ready. She can either limit her time there or find ways to deal with things as they happen. When she knows that busy places increase her anxiety, she can better plan her reaction and handle it with tools that assist her.

Triggers can be minor or hidden. There may not be a clear reason why certain patterns in clothes or sudden changes in her routine make your daughter anxious. A useful way to see trends over time is to help her keep a journal or even just a list of times when she feels nervous. Keeping this book will help you identify places and events that make you unhappy. Once she knows what sets off her worries, she won't be as surprised by them and can deal with them on her own.

A famous autism expert named Dr. Tony Attwood has said, "Understanding why can be as significant as knowing how." For your daughter, just being aware of what sets off her emotions is a powerful form of self-knowledge that gives her control over them. When she learns about these things that make her anxious, she's no longer powerless over them; she can face them with knowledge and courage.

Make Your Daughter a Customized Anxiety Toolkit

Once your daughter knows what makes her anxious, the next step is to help her deal with it when it happens. This is done by giving her techniques and tools. She can use these tools whenever she needs them. Think of them as her own personal resources. All of the things in her toolkit should really help her feel better and more like herself. These tools could be things that stimulate her senses, activities that calm her down, or breathing and awareness techniques—anything that makes her feel safe and in charge when her anxiety rises.

Start putting together this toolkit by being honest with her about what calms her down. For some girls, sensory tools like worry balls or fabrics with different textures can be very relaxing and help them get rid of their nervous energy. Some people may like noise-canceling headphones to block out loud sounds, especially when in a busy place. Having a soft, familiar blanket for my daughter to cling to during stressful times was immensely beneficial. It was like a "safety net" for her, something she could depend on when she was struggling.

Another strong tool that can help her kit is breathing techniques. Simple practices, such as the 4-7-8 method (inhale for four beats, hold for seven, exhale for eight), can help her control how her body reacts to stress. Tell her to try these skills when she's not anxious so they are easy to use when she is. As she gets better at these exercises, she may automatically turn to them whenever worry rises.

Don't forget how significant creativity is. Making art, writing a book, or even just listening to music can be very healing. She might find that they become some of her favorite ways to deal with nervousness. If she likes to draw, for example, carrying a small sketchbook with her can make her work with stress by doing something artistic and pleasant. Some girls find that these kinds of creative outlets not only help them deal with their stress at the time. They also help them understand and process their feelings over time.

Let her know that it's okay to modify this toolkit as she grows and you work together. Changes in her needs are a positive sign because it means she's learning more about herself and how to thrive in new ways. One of the greatest things we can do, according to Dr. Brené Brown, is to own our story and love ourselves through it. By giving her this toolkit, you're giving her the power to own her story, which includes worry but is not defined by it.

Why routines can help you deal with daily stress

Autistic girls require routines, not only for their comfort. Routines make things more predictable and give her a way to depend on order in a world that can feel crazy or too much to handle. Making daily habits can help her deal with stress by giving her a sense of security and control. She can move about her day with more confidence if she knows what to expect. Her worry is less likely to become more intense if something unexpected happens.

Set up patterns for key times in her day, like in the morning, after school, or before bed. For instance, if she usually has a difficult time getting up in the morning, set up a routine of things she can do every day. Some activities that could be included on this list include having a peaceful breakfast, engaging in deep breathing or stretching exercises, and consistently keeping prepared in the same order each day. This steady flow can help her get ready for the day and make her feel less anxious when she wakes up.

Her routine also helps her deal with changes, which can be challenging at times. It can be difficult to switch activities, especially if the settings or standards differ. Having small routines ready for these situations can facilitate changes easier. Sometimes it's challenging for her to switch from schoolwork to fun. She can adjust to the upcoming activity more easily with a short routine, such as taking a few deep breaths or listening to her favorite song.

One mom said that her daughter had a difficult time traveling from school to home at the end of the day. She found comfort in a simple routine: every day after school, they stopped at a quiet park for five minutes before returning home. This regular routine gave her daughter a chance to relax, acting as a bridge between school and home, where she had more freedom. Over time, this routine became an integral part of their routine, significantly reducing her daughter's anxiety about returning home from school.

Setting habits doesn't mean you can't be flexible; life will always surprise you, and you should teach her that she can be flexible and follow a pattern at the same time. You might even want to include a "backup plan" in case things don't work out as planned. This could mean having a comforting toy or activity ready for unexpected events. This will help her deal with changes in a realistic way. Routines can give her strength because they help her plan for what's next, but learning how to deal with changes gives her the strength to handle life's shocks.

<u>Change and Introspection</u>

You're giving your daughter the tools to deal with anxiety and emotional overwhelm. This is done by helping her figure out her triggers, making a custom anxiety toolkit, and setting up healthy habits. Take a moment to think about these ideas: What in her life triggers her? How could a toolbox for worry assist her during challenging times? What habits can you help her form to enhance her day's stability?

Now that you know these basics, let's look at "What to Do About Rejection Sensitivity."

WHAT TO DO IF YOU FEEL SENSITIVE TO REJECTION?

She alters her perspective on negative social encounters.

It can be very painful to feel rejected, especially for autistic girls who may already feel different from their peers. Every negative social experience, regardless of its magnitude, has the potential to intensify, akin to a wound that requires a prolonged healing process. To help your daughter deal with her feelings of rejection, learning how to rethink these events can be very helpful. Instead of seeing these times as proof that there is something "wrong" with her, she can learn to see them as normal parts of life. Although this shift in perspective won't alleviate her feelings, it can assist her in understanding that rejection doesn't imply inadequacy.

Let's say she had a negative experience at school. Perhaps a friend failed to invite her to a party, or someone said something that upset her. Instead of making assumptions about what happened, you should encourage her to ask questions such as "What could be the other person's point of view?" or "Is it possible that what they did has nothing to do with me?" By considering alternative scenarios, she can begin to comprehend that rejection doesn't necessarily indicate a flaw in her character. This new way of looking at things helps her understand that social relationships are complicated and that people's actions are often caused by their own emotions or situations, not their opinion of her worth.

Sharing some of your own rejection stories can help you understand this idea better. Discuss a moment when you didn't feel included or understood, and how it took you some time to realize that those feelings didn't shape who you are today. Describe a moment when altering your perspective on rejection facilitated personal growth or imparted valuable lessons. To feel better, she can remember that rejection is something everyone experiences and doesn't have to be permanent or personal.

Dr. Carol Dweck, who is famous for her work on the growth mindset, says, "We can grow through difficulty if we see challenges as chances to learn and get better." This way of thinking works exceptionally well when it comes to social situations. It can be life-changing to help her see negative exchanges as chances to grow instead of signs that she has failed. She'll get stronger over time and be able to handle rejection, knowing that it hurts but doesn't have to define her.

Support and validation can help you build emotional strength.

It takes time to become emotionally strong, especially for someone who feels rejected a lot. For your daughter to become more resilient, she needs to be in a caring setting where she feels seen, heard, and accepted. It's not okay to play down her pain or tell her to "just get over it." Instead, tell her her feelings are real and understandable, even if the cause may not matter to others. By confirming what she has said, you build trust and security that will help her face future obstacles with more confidence.

Imagine that she is visibly upset when she gets home from school because she feels neglected by her peers. Instead of giving her help or answers right away, acknowledge her feelings: "I can see that you're really frustrated." "That must have been challenging." Just hearing that can make a huge difference. It lets her know that her emotions are valid and that it's okay to be upset or hurt. She may need to talk about how she feels sometimes without fixing anything right away. When you listen to her without judging, it shows that you value her feelings and give her a safe place to work through them.

After making her feel heard and understood, you can gently help her see things in a more general way. One question you could pose is, "Has this experience taught you anything about yourself or other people?" or "What do you think will make you be better the next time this happens?" These questions encourage her to think about her feelings without ignoring them. She will learn that being emotionally strong doesn't mean escaping pain; it means knowing she can deal with problems and feel better with help and self-compassion.

Getting stronger takes time, but the trip is worth it. You can choose not to let circumstances bring you down, but some are out of your control. Teaching your daughter to feel her feelings without letting them define her will help her stand tall even in tough social settings. She will get stronger with each experience and gain the courage to handle anything that comes her way with strength and self-assurance.

We teach students how to deal with criticism confidently.

If you are sensitive to rejection, criticism, even if it is constructive, can feel like a blow. Girls with autism often struggle with their self-esteem daily, making criticism feel particularly personal and distressing. Teaching your daughter how to take criticism healthy is a skill that will serve her for the rest of her life. If she doesn't see feedback as a sign of how excellent she is, she can learn to see it as a way to improve herself or even something to just let go of if it's not valuable.

First, help her understand the difference between helpful and harmful criticism. Criticism that is meant to aid her get better comes from love, even if it's uncomfortable to hear at times. Criticism that doesn't help, on the other hand, usually arises from people's opinions or mistakes. Tell her that she can choose which complaints to pay attention to and which to ignore. When you provide her with feedback, instruct her to ask herself questions such as "Is this criticism meant to enable me to grow?" or "Does this come from someone I know and trust?" These questions encourage her to think critically about feedback, which gives her more power over how it affects her.

Let's imagine she receives feedback on a school project she worked hard on. She gets upset when her teacher tells her she needs to work on something because she thinks it means she didn't do a decent job. Tell her to pay attention to the specific ideas and ask herself, "How can I utilize this feedback to improve my work even more?" Say to her again that positive criticism is a beneficial way to learn and grow, and that not just the smartest people can take advantage of it.

Help her see feedback as something she can use or throw away. This method keeps her in control and teaches her that feedback is valuable, but it doesn't determine its importance. Let me know how you've handled criticism, even if it means ignoring it. Using personal stories can help her understand and feel better about these lessons, letting her know she's not the only one who struggles with criticism.

"Daring to set boundaries is about having the courage to love ourselves, even when we risk disappointing others," says Dr. Brené Brown, an expert on vulnerability and courage. Teaching her to tell the difference between positive feedback and hurtful criticism boosts her self-esteem and gives her the confidence to set emotional boundaries. She will learn to accept criticism as something that can help her grow or that doesn't matter.

<u>Change and Introspection</u>

You're giving her the tools to face the world with confidence. This is done by helping her reframe social events, building emotional strength, and showing her how to deal with criticism. Think about how these tools could benefit her in her daily life. For example, how could rethinking adverse events make her less sensitive to rejection? How can you help her support herself? What role does confidence in feedback play in her journey?

Now that we have these tools, let's look at how to deal with "Tools to Manage Sensory Overload."

Ways to Handle Too Many Sensory Experiences

If you have sensory overload, it can feel like many sights, sounds, and feelings come at you all at once. Noise and visual inputs can quickly be too much for your daughter, making it challenging for her to concentrate, think clearly, or feel at ease. Hearing aids and vision aids can help her by blocking out noise and giving her more control over her sensory surroundings. These tools aim to facilitate her connection with the world in a manner that suits her.

Imagine that your daughter is in a school cafeteria that is very noisy. This is with trays crashing against each other, talks taking place on at the same time, and a steady hum of activity. It can be difficult to breathe through this overwhelming chaos. She can focus on her thoughts without distraction by using noise-canceling headphones. There are headphones that completely block out sound and headphones that let her choose how much sound she wants to let in. If you give her this choice, she might feel more in control of her sensory information.

Visual aids like sunglasses or brimmed hats can also reduce excitement. Visual overload can happen in places with lots of people, bright lights, and rapid movements. Wearing colored glasses or a comfortable hat can lessen the brightness of bright rooms. This makes it easier for her to move around in places that are exciting for the eyes. I recall a mother who gifted her daughter with a stylish pair of tinted glasses that she would find useful but also enjoyable to wear.

She transformed the sensory tool into an effective and powerful instrument.

These gadgets are not to isolate her but to create a sensory environment that enhances her performance. Temple Grandin, a famous autistic advocate who knows a lot about how our senses work, once said, "We have to find things that work for each individual's physical needs." Giving your daughter the tools to control her visual input will help her participate in more of her daily activities without feeling overwhelmed all the time.

Introducing clothes and textures beneficial for sensitive skin

Clothing might not seem relevant, but for someone with sensory issues, what they choose can make a big difference in how at ease they can be. It can be difficult to get dressed if the clothes are scratchy, the waistbands are too tight, or the tags rub against your skin. Added clothes and patterns suitable for sensitive skin can change a person's whole life, turning a daily struggle into a chance to become more relaxed and confident. She wears these clothes not for fashion but to look comfortable in her own skin.

She might be fussy about clothes and refuse to wear certain outfits because they "don't seem right." Sensory-friendly clothes can help with these problems by having soft fabrics, seamless patterns, and fewer tags or labels. Some brands offer pants made of smooth, stretchy material that feels like a second skin and t-shirts with flat seams that don't irritate sensitive areas. She should be able to help you select items based on what she finds comfortable. Since she feels comfortable in her clothes, she's more likely to be brave in public.

When I worked with one family, their daughter wouldn't wear jeans because of stiff material and rough seams. Getting dressed in the morning used to be challenging, but after moving to soft clothes like cotton pants and tagless shirts, it became simple and stress-free. Her parents say she felt differently. When she wasn't in pain, she seemed calmer and ready for the day.

Textures aren't just found on clothes. Consider incorporating sensory-friendly furniture, such as weighted blankets or soft, flexible sheets, to create a comfortable and restful space. Weighted blankets help her relax after a long day by applying gentle pressure that calms her down. Everything, from her clothes to the fabrics she sleeps in, aims to calm her senses rather than overwhelm them.

By putting safety first, you're telling her that her emotional needs are paramount and that it's okay to do what helps her feel comfortable. This method not only makes her life easier, but also teaches her to pay attention to her body and meet her own wants. An expert on sensory processing, Dr. Winnie Dunn, says, "When we change our environments to support sensory preferences, we make it possible for people to feel safe and secure." In this way, clothing is more than just fabric; it's a way to bring people together.

Taking breaks to move can calm down overactive senses.

She may feel trapped in a loop of too much input and unable to calm down when experiencing sensory overload. Taking breaks to move around can help her reset her senses and let out pent-up energy. Not only do these breaks help her release excess energy, but they also provide a respite from her worries and aid her return to a tranquil state of mind.

Imagine she is in a busy school day. The noise, the people around her, and the constant changes in activities all add up, making her feel tense. For example, a short walk down the hall, some stretching, or light dancing on a yoga ball can give her the physical release she needs to work through her feelings and calm down again. She can use her body's stress reaction to do something physical, which helps her feel grounded instead of overwhelmed.

She can plan these breaks or take them whenever she wants, whichever works best for her. If she is aware of her school's sensory overload plan and appears to be reaching her limits, her teacher might consider granting her a movement break. You can get her moving every day at home by stretching in the morning or having a quick dance party before she starts her homework. By making these breaks a regular part of her day, she will learn that it's okay to stop, step back, and take care of herself when she needs it.

When stressed or overstimulated, a mom I know found that her daughter did well when she jumped on a small trampoline. Her racing thoughts calmed down, and the repeated action helped her get back in touch with her body. Over time, these breaks became a vital part of their daily routine. They provided her daughter with a consistent method of managing her emotional stress through physical activity.

Moving around during breaks teaches her to control her emotional experience. She doesn't have to stay stressed out—even small things can help her feel better. Patricia Wilbarger, an occupational therapist who specializes in sensory integration, says, "Movement is the key to sensory integration." By using movement as a tool, you give her a way to stay in touch with her body and emotions and help her become more resilient against emotional overload.

<u>Change and Introspection</u>

You provide her with the necessary tools to manage her sensory overload. These tools include noise-cancelling headphones, clothes that are easy on the senses, and breaks to move around. Think about how these tools can help her. What sights or sounds cause her to be overwhelmed most by them? What alterations to her attire or surroundings could improve her mood? What types of breaks could she take to move around that would be enjoyable and appropriate for her?

Once you've implemented these strategies, let's explore "How to Create a Calming Environment She Loves."

HOW CAN I CREATE A RELAXING SPACE THAT SHE LOVES?

She is assembling a sensory sanctuary using her preferred tranquil objects.

A calm place can be a safe haven where your daughter feels completely at ease and protected. Imagine making her a sensory hideaway with all of her favorite relaxing things. She could retreat there when the world becomes too overwhelming for her. It doesn't have to be a big change; small changes that fit her tastes can make a big difference. A sensory getaway is about creating a space that meets her needs and tastes. This is so she can relax and recharge in a way that feels natural and safe.

Start by focusing on the sights, sounds, and things that bring her comfort. Soft, fluffy fabrics, adorned with a variety of pillows or blankets, provide a tactile sensation that some children find comforting. Some people feel more grounded when smelling soft scents like vanilla or lavender. You can incorporate these scents into your space by using essential oil diffusers or light-scented cloth sprays. In the past, I worked with a young girl who found comfort in wool and cotton. Her parents created a cozy space for her, complete with wool blankets, beanbags, and pillows. This was where she could curl up with a book or unwind.

You might want to make her escape more sensory-friendly by setting up different "zones." It might be beneficial to have dim lighting and soft blankets in one spot to help you relax. You could place stress balls or other items with different textures in a separate room. This will allow her to use her senses without becoming overwhelmed. A sensory getaway isn't a space that works for everyone; it's her own safe place made to support and soothe her specific physical needs. Including these elements affirms her right to a space that prioritizes her happiness and allows her to express herself without fear of judgment.

Temple Grandin, a famous autism supporter, once said, "The world needs all kinds of minds." Giving her a safe place to visit that takes into account her physical preferences will help her feel like her needs are meaningful and real. A sensory getaway soothes her feelings and makes her feel like she belongs. This reminds her that there is a special place that knows and loves her.

How lighting, colors, and sounds can make you feel at ease

A lot of what makes us feel at ease in a place is its lighting, colors, and sounds. All of these physical things can affect your daughter's getaway mood. Bright lights, loud noises, or harsh colors can be upsetting. On the other hand, soft lighting, calming colors, and soft sounds can help create a calm and relaxing space. By adding thoughtful sensory elements to her room, you give her power over it and lower the risk of sensory overload.

First, let's talk about light. You might want to replace your bright ceiling lights with lamps or string lights that glow warm and cozy. Also, natural light can be helpful, so if her room has windows, think about how to make the most of the sun. She can control how bright the room is by adding blackout shades, which is especially helpful if she is sensitive to light. There was a mom I worked with whose daughter found comfort in a small LED lamp that changed colors. For peace and quiet, she could pick soft blue or green shades. When she wanted to read, she could turn on a brighter light. Giving her the power to turn on the lights lets her adjust her space to fit her needs and feelings.

Colors can also evoke emotions in you. While bright reds and oranges can wake you up, they may be too exciting for relaxation. Soft colors like blues, greens, and pastels calm people down and create a relaxing visual setting. She can change the mood of her space by painting one wall her favorite soothing color or adding soft-colored blankets. Small changes can make a big difference, so you don't have to redo the whole room.

We can also alter the sound to improve her mood. Soundscapes made of white noise, nature sounds, or soothing music can help her rest by creating a calm setting. I once met a mom who played soft ocean sounds in her daughter's room with the lights off. It was relaxing to read, do homework, or just relax with the sounds. The sounds in her room helped her feel stable and calm, which made her less likely to become agitated.

Putting together a place for her that has the right lighting, colors, and sounds is more than just making her feel comfortable physically; it also meets her emotional needs. An expert on sensory processing, Dr. Winnie Dunn, says, "When we change environments to meet sensory needs, we support well-being and foster resilience." Making these changes to her space isn't just about looks; it's about making it a safe and comforting place for her.

We are collaborating with her to create a distinctive space.

With your daughter, making her room her own is one of the most effective ways to calm her down. Allowing her to make choices about her surroundings teaches her that her choices matter. This empowers her to transform her world to suit her needs. It's not enough to decorate a room; she needs to create a safe place that fits her personality and lets her feel happy.

Start by letting her help with every part of the process, from picking out fabrics and colors to picking out sensory tools and decorations. You could ask her questions such as "What colors make you feel calm?" or "Do you like the idea of a room with dim lights or bright ones?" These questions will help her think about what she really wants from her place, even if she doesn't have an answer right away. She'll become more clear about what she wants over time, and you'll help her make the place feel like her own.

From the type of rug to the pattern of the curtains, the mother I worked with let her daughter choose everything. Her daughter picked soft blues and greens, pictures of her favorite animals, and a beanbag-filled reading nook. When she finished, the room became more than just a place to be; it evolved into a reflection of her identity. She felt like she owned and was proud of the place she created because of the choices she made. It became an extension of who she was.

Personalizing her space also helps her express herself. Encourage her to incorporate items that hold special meaning for her, such as her own artwork, photographs of her loved ones, or items from her hobbies. These things are more than just decorations; they represent her unique personality and help her remember what makes her joyful and calm. It's not just a place for her to relax; her room becomes a place where she can enjoy who she is, filled with things that bring her contentment and calm.

"Owning our story and loving ourselves through that process is the bravest thing we'll ever do," said Dr. Brené Brown. Making her space unique is a small but significant way for her to own her story. When you work together in her room, you're not only giving her a place to relax, but also providing her with little boosts of confidence as you progress.

<u>Change and Introspection</u>

You're helping her come up with a relaxing place that feels like home by planning a sensory retreat. This is done with carefully chosen lighting, colors, and sounds. You're also giving her the freedom to make it her own. When you consider these aspects of her life, what calming elements could improve her mood? How can the colors and lights you choose make you feel better? And how can working with others in her space help her accept who she is?

Now that you know these ways to relax better, let's look at "Easy Mindfulness Tricks for Everyday Stress."

Simple Ways to Handle Stress Everyday

Everyone breathes every day without thinking about it, but when you do it on purpose, it can relax your mind and body. Simple breathing techniques can make a huge difference for your daughter. They can help her calm down when she feels stressed or overloaded. Teaching her how to control her breath is like giving her a "reset" button to feel calm anywhere and at any time.

Begin with something easy, like the 4-7-8 breathing method. For this, you need to breathe in for four counts, hold your breath for seven counts, and breathe out for eight counts. Slowly walk her through the steps and let her practice at her own speed. Tell her the point is to focus on her breath rhythm, not perfection. She will feel calmer when she does this exercise over time, knowing she has a way to deal with her worry right now.

Let's say she's getting nervous as she prepares to talk in class. The 4-7-8 method allows her to slow down, gain ground, and concentrate on the task at hand without excessive stress. This exercise can become her go-to way to calm down even when things aren't very problematic, like right before bed or when she's feeling stressed at home. One mom I worked with did this every night before bed with her daughter. It became a bonding activity that helped them both feel better. After practicing this technique with her every day, her daughter gained the confidence to use it independently whenever she felt nervous.

If it's challenging for your daughter to keep track of counts, try an easier way, like deep belly breathing. She does this by putting her hands on her belly and letting it rise as she breathes in deeply and fall as she breathes out. Focusing on the breath and working the diaphragm while belly breathing makes you feel relaxed. To do these routines, all you need are a few minutes and a quiet place to relax.

"Proper breathing is a fundamental tool in the reduction of stress and anxiety," says Dr. Andrew Weil, a doctor known for his work in integrative medicine. Teaching her these techniques gives her the power to control how her body reacts to stress and reminds her that she can find calm in any situation.

Use guided imagery to create a safe space in your mind.

Guided imagery is a wonderful way to help your daughter get away from things that make her feel stressed. It gives her a mental safe space whenever she needs to. In this method, she uses her mind to picture a quiet place, like a beach, a forest, or even a cozy room. This is where she knows she is safe and at ease. Guided images, while still gentle, can redirect her focus to a sense of inner calm.

To get her to think about this idea, ask her to name a place that makes her feel happy. Talk about it: What does she see? What sounds does she hear? How does the air smell? You can help her visualize her mental safe place in excellent detail by telling her to use all her senses when she visualizes it. Sometimes she pictures soft waves, the sun on her skin, or soft grass under her feet. The more clearly she can picture this space in her mind, the better it will work to calm her down.

A family I know instructed their daughter in guided imagery because she loved the outdoors and wildlife. Together, they imagined a quiet jungle where she could sit with peaceful animals, with trees all around her and sunlight coming through the leaves. When she felt stressed, she would close her eyes, inhale deeply, and visualize herself in her "forest." The calm would then wash over her. This easy method became her center and helped her feel in charge of her emotions.

To make guided imagery even easier for her to use, you could record a brief audio guide about her safe place. She can listen to it whenever she needs peace. Knowing she has a safe place to rest in her mind can give her peace, especially when things get too much for her. Mindfulness expert Dr. Jon Kabat-Zinn says, "You can't stop the waves, but you can learn to surf." Guided imagery doesn't get rid of stress, but it helps you deal with it peacefully.

Mindfulness doesn't have to be a separate practice; it can be a part of her daily life by incorporating it into her habits. Your daughter can build a lasting sense of calm and presence by practicing mindfulness during everyday tasks. This can be very helpful in dealing with stress. She needs to be able to connect with the present moment while she eats, brushes her teeth, or gets ready for bed.

Start your day with something thoughtful. Do not forget to notice how her body responds to awakening. Have her take a few deep breaths. As she stands up, tell her to pay attention to how her feet feel on the floor. Tell her how the water feels on her skin as she washes her face, and how her breakfast tastes. She learns to stay in the present moment by focusing on these small physical experiences. This makes it less likely for her mind to wander to anxious thoughts.

Mindfulness is also beneficial while eating. Encourage her to enjoy her food's tastes, textures, and colors for a short time. Instead of organizing it, get her to enjoy every bite and notice how the tastes and textures change. Mindfulness during meals helps her develop the habit of taking things slowly. This can assist her deal with problems in other areas of her life with a calm, steady presence.

I remember a family who took their daughter for a thoughtful walk after dinner. As they strolled leisurely through the neighborhood, they identified an intriguing sight or sound. For example, the sound of leaves shifting or the scent of freshly cut grass. She loved going for walks because they allowed her to relax and connect with her surroundings. These small things helped her learn to be at peace with the present moment without doing anything else.

Mindfulness helps her find peace of mind anywhere and at any time. Thought teacher Thich Nhat Hanh says, "The present moment is full of joy and happiness." "If you pay attention, you will see it." By practicing mindfulness in easy-to-understand ways, your daughter develops the ability to find balance in life's stressful situations.

<u>Change and Introspection</u>

You're giving her tools to deal with normal stress by teaching her breathing exercises, guided imagery, and ways to incorporate awareness into her daily life. Think about how these practices could help her. Which breathing method could she use most often? How does guided thought make your mind feel safe? Could mindfulness calm any aspect of her daily life?

Now that you have these careful methods in place, let's talk about "Helping Your Daughter Learn to Self-Regulate."

How to Teach Your Daughter to Control Herself

She is figuring out what makes her feel down.

Everyone experiences complex emotions, but your daughter may experience them more intensely than others at times. The first step in teaching her to self-regulate is to help her figure out what triggers her to feel unwell. Emotional triggers are things, people, or events that make you respond very strongly, and they often do so without notice. She will be better able to deal with these triggers in a safe and controlled way if she learns to spot them.

Take a moment to picture your daughter in a busy, noisy place like a grocery store. She could feel worried or frustrated without knowing why. The sounds of people talking and the presence of a large crowd can trigger overwhelm and frustration. Finding these triggers ahead of time will help her understand what makes her feel uneasy. This will allow her to prepare or avoid things that make her uneasy and stressed.

It might help to keep a "trigger journal" in this case. Encourage her to write down times when she becomes very upset or stressed. What did she do before her thoughts strengthened? Was there a certain sound, sight, or talk that set it off? Over time, patterns may show up that will enable her to understand her mental environment better. For example, she may discover that certain changes, such as transitioning from school to home, often trigger her anxiety. Once she knows this, she can plan how to handle the changes with more help and preparation.

This process can seem easier if you use examples from your own life. You could say, "Being late makes me anxious; it makes me feel out of control." Letting her know that everyone has their own triggers can help her feel a lot less alone. A psychologist named Dr. Susan David, who is known for her work on emotional agility, says, "Understanding our triggers is the first step to implementing choices rather than just reacting." By assisting her in comprehending her triggers, you empower her to come up with informed decisions about how to respond to them, preventing unexpected surprises.

Put together a step-by-step self-control plan

The next step is to make a self-regulation plan that fits her needs once she has a better idea of what sets her off. This plan is like a personal road map that shows her how to calm down and get back in charge whenever she feels stressed. Setting up a structured way to control her feelings doesn't just help her in the present; it also gives her more trust in her ability to deal with them in the future. Because she knows she has a plan, she can control her thoughts instead of letting them take over.

First, break down the self-regulation plan into clear steps she can implement when she starts to sense an emotional response coming on. The first thing she might need to do is admit she's feeling too much. To do this, she might need to notice physical signs, such as a racing heartbeat or sweaty hands. The second step could be to do something that makes you feel better. This could be taking a few deep breaths, being outside for a short time, or engaging in a fidget toy. Every part of the plan is a small goal that helps her focus on one thing at a time instead of overwhelming feelings.

A family I know devised a simple plan for their daughter, who experiences anxiety in social situations. She would take three deep breaths, try to find a quiet place to sit for a while, and use a centering method. For example, touching something small in her pocket. This plan was very useful for her, and it was simple enough to follow anywhere. Having a set list of steps to follow gave her order when things felt chaotic otherwise.

Let her help you create the plan; that way it will feel unique to her. Ask her what makes her feel calm, what steps she'd like to take, and what order works for her senses. By being involved, she makes sure the plan works and shows she cares about it. Child expert Dr. Ross Greene once said, "Kids do well if they can." By creating a plan, you equip her with the necessary tools and confidence to manage her emotions effectively.

Visual tools to keep track of and handle emotions

Visual aids can really help your daughter understand, keep track of, and control her feelings. A lot of kids find it easier to talk about how they feel when they can see it on a picture, like a chart, a color, or a sign. Help her find patterns over time by giving her a way to clearly track her feelings. This will make her feel more in control.

The "feeling thermometer" is a popular way to keep track of your feelings visually. This chart has colors that run from cool and calm at the bottom to warm and intense at the top. Each color represents a different emotional intensity. At any time, she can use the temperature to show how she's feeling. She might point to a cool color if she's worried and a hot color near the top if she's really stressed. This simple tool helps her figure out how she's feeling and gives her a way to convey how she wants without words. This can be especially helpful if she has trouble expressing herself verbally.

A mood or "Emotion Wheel" is another choice. Each section of this chart shows a different feeling or mood. She can take a moment at the end of each day to think about the day and color in the part that most accurately describes how she felt. Over time, trends may show up that will enable you both to understand how she feels. There's a chance she gets stressed out on Mondays or enjoys alone time the most. Knowing this helps you both prepare for high stress and find better ways to support her.

A mom I know made her daughter a "Feelings Journal" where she drew simple faces to show how she was feeling, like happy, unhappy, angry, or calm. Daily, her daughter circled the face that showed how she felt and sometimes wrote down what made her think that way. The log was helpful because it showed which days and events affected people in different ways. This visual input gave her daughter the confidence to talk more freely about how she was feeling. This is because she had a real way to explain what she had been through.

"Feelings come and go like clouds in a windy sky," said Thich Nhat Hanh, a master of mindfulness. "Conscious breathing is my anchor." Teaching her to picture and keep track of her feelings helps her see that they are only brief and can be handled. She can keep an eye on her feelings without becoming upset by using tools like the thermometer, wheel, or journal. This makes her feel in charge and helps her understand herself better.

<u>Change and Introspection</u>

You're teaching her lasting skills for emotional resilience and awareness by helping her figure out what causes her to feel bad. You're establishing a personalized plan for self-regulation and keeping track of her feelings visually. Think about how these methods fit her specific needs. What are the most common causes you've seen? Which self-regulation steps make sense to her? And how might tools for visual tracking make it easier for her to understand how she's feeling?

Now that you know how to control yourself, let's talk about "How to Talk About Periods and Body Changes Without Being Awkward."

Chapter 3: Growing Up with Autism

"Growth is the great separator between those who succeed and those who do not. When I see a person beginning to separate themselves from the pack, it's almost always due to personal growth." – John C. Maxwell

How to Talk About Your Period and Body Changes Without Being Stuck Up

We should make puberty clear and simple.

Young girls can find puberty scary, but using simple, direct language can help your daughter feel better. Don't use euphemisms or unclear words. Instead, be clear and direct so she understands her body. You want to make things clear and reassure her that she doesn't need to be afraid of puberty. This is because it's a normal part of growing up.

Start with straightforward things. Tell her that everyone passes through puberty, which is when their bodies change to look more like adults'. You could say something like, "Your body will change in different ways during puberty." Your period, which is when you shed a little blood each month, is caused by growing parts of your body. Use simple language, and don't include too many technical terms unless she's comfortable with them. Assure her that these changes are normal and expected.

One mother I know used a simple calendar to talk to her daughter about periods. She showed what a "cycle" looks like and talked about how the body gets ready every month. This helped her daughter picture and understand when her period would come, making the idea less abstract and more real. Seeing and hearing it broken down took the mystery out of the process and gave her a better sense of what to expect.

If she seems lost, use comparisons that make sense to her. For example, telling her that her body changes and grows over time like a plant could help her understand that growth is a normal process that happens over time. "Kids need clarity as much as reassurance," says Dr. Lisa Damour, a clinical psychologist who works with teens. By keeping your answers simple and straight, you'll help her feel strong instead of nervous as her body changes.

It's acceptable to inquire about her body and discuss it.

To help her understand how her body is changing, it is imperative to make her feel safe enough to ask questions and have open talks. Ensure she understands that she can ask any "weird" or "wrong" questions about her body without fear of judgment. Being honest with her like this not only helps her learn, but also builds confidence by showing her that she can talk to you whenever she's not sure what to do.

Let's say she wants to know why periods happen. You could say, "That's an awesome question, and I'm so glad you contacted me!" instead of giving a quick answer. Then, you could explain that menstruation is a natural way for the body to prepare for having children in the future. If she's not ready, this answer doesn't have to go into detail about reproduction. The intention is to pique her curiosity while allowing further inquiries.

Make time for these kinds of talks in casual, laid-back places. It can be less scary to discuss on a walk or in a quiet moment at home than to sit down for a "serious talk." For example, one mother I worked with would have light chats with her daughter over tea in the evening, which felt safe and comfortable. This made her daughter feel comfortable asking questions without being embarrassed. It became clear to her that talking about her body was everyday and not a big deal.

By making these talks seem normal, you're teaching her and giving her the courage to own her experiences. And she'll become stronger and less nervous when she realizes that talking about her body is just like talking about anything else. Body-positive activist Jameela Jamil says our bodies are extraordinary and deserve understanding and respect. Letting her ask questions and talk about how she feels helps her have a healthy, open relationship with her body as it changes.

We provide her with helpful tools and information to prepare her.

While knowledge is incredibly valuable, it's equally critical to feel prepared by having useful tools and resources available. For example, helping her put together a kit for her period can give her the confidence to handle this new situation. Her "just-in-case" tools can be a small bag with pads, wipes, and an extra pair of underwear. This will give her peace of mind when her period starts, whether she's at home or out and about.

Talk to her about the different options, like pads, tampons, or period cups, and show her how to use these things. This way, she will realize she is aware and in charge of her choices. Start with the choice that makes her feel most at ease before explaining others. You could show her how to attach a pad to her underwear, for example, and let her practice at home in a low-stakes setting. They don't want to scare her, but make her feel safe. She'll become less nervous and more ready once she knows these things.

Giving her books or other tools for her age can also be helpful. Some kids learn best through pictures and stories, so a book that talks about puberty in a fun, easy-to-understand way can accompany along with your talks. A mother I know gave her daughter a beautifully drawn book about puberty. It talked about periods and body changes in a polite and interesting way. Her daughter felt more educated and involved in the process. This is because she knew that these changes were common and that many people would journey through them too.

Giving her useful information makes her feel confident she can handle what's coming. "Knowledge is power," says Brené Brown, an expert on openness and courage. She will replace her worry about body changes with quiet trust in her own abilities when she feels ready.

<u>Change and Introspection</u>

You can build confidence and knowledge around puberty and body changes by using clear language, making questions seem normal, and giving useful tools. Think about how these tactics might help her on her trip. Are there parts where she needs more information? What sorts of things can you ask her to put her at ease? And how can getting ready for these changes in the real world enable her feel confident?

Now that we have these helpful tools, let's look at "Boosting Her Body Image in a Way That Works."

WE AIM TO MAKE HER APPRECIATE HER BODY FUNCTIONALLY.

Focusing on her body's capabilities rather than its appearance can significantly boost her confidence in a society that often prioritizes appearance.

Encouraging your daughter to prioritize her body's capabilities over its appearance can significantly enhance her confidence in a society that constantly emphasizes appearances. When she values her body for its strength, toughness, and skills, she is less likely to let what others think define her. You give her a sense of self-worth that extends beyond how she looks by focusing on what her body allows her to do.

To begin, let's celebrate what her body can do. Can she play her favorite sport, climb trees, or dance to her favorite song? Tell her that these things are signs of her special power. For example, if she enjoys swimming, highlight her strength and coordination between her arms and legs. Also, tell her how her lungs help her breathe deeply and stay stable. This method can help her feel grateful for her body's abilities, seeing it as a wonderful tool that enables her to do the things she loves.

A family I know sparked their daughter's interest in climbing, teaching her to appreciate her legs and lungs by carrying her up steep hills. They celebrated every hill they climbed and every mile they ran as an adventure that showcased her strength. Instead of how she looked, she became proud of her body for what it could do. This pride fostered a positive relationship with her body, independent of external beauty standards.

You can help her focus on her abilities instead of her looks by telling her to think of her body as something that lets her explore, create, and experience life. To quote Olympian and body-positive activist Allyson Felix, "Strength is showing up and being brave enough to embrace the body you have." Helping your daughter see her body as a source of strength will teach her that her worth isn't just skin deep, but in the things her body makes possible.

You can combat media and peer pressure by utilizing positive role models.

The things that the media and her friends say about her can affect how she sees herself. TV, newspapers, and even movies often propagate a narrow and false idea of beauty. This can lead to feelings of inadequacy and self-worth. A strong way to support her body image is to help her deal with these pressures by presenting her to a variety of positive role models. When she sees strong, confident women who prioritize authenticity over appearance, she learns that beauty extends beyond what society perceives.

You could put her in touch with sports, artists, scientists, or organizers who are proud of who they are. They focus on their interests instead of their looks. You could show her figures of body-positive people like Serena Williams, who sees her muscles as a source of strength, or Ashley Graham, a model and author who defies beauty standards by loving her body just the way it is. These women serve as real-life examples of women valued for their skills, knowledge, and self-confidence, rather than just their physical appearance.

I know another mom who told her daughter to follow social media accounts that support health, body confidence, and accepting herself. They each picked an account that celebrates variety and shares stories of women of all shapes and sizes who are doing well. This helped her daughter see a wider range of beauty and understand that worth isn't based on how someone appears over time. When she felt like she had to meet certain beauty standards, she thought of the women she loved. She would remember that confidence isn't just about looks.

Tell her to contemplate about the things she learns and hears in the media. Every time she sees an advertisement for a " flawless " body, ask her, "Do you think everyone looks like that?" What makes a person strong or beautiful besides how they look? Teaching her to think critically gives her the tools to survive a world full of false perceptions. An organizer and founder of the "I Weigh" movement, Jameela Jamil, says, "Your body is not your enemy; your body is your home." By demonstrating to her that there are many ways to be happy and feel positive about yourself, you help her understand this truth.

Encourage individuals to express themselves through art, fashion, or hobbies.

A fun and powerful way to help your daughter feel positive about her body is to let her express herself. When she has fashion, art, or other hobbies that let her explore her personality, she values her uniqueness. She finds ways to express herself that inspire her feel happy. Self-expression helps her become more comfortable in her own skin because it allows her to see her body as a blank surface for art instead of something to compare it to.

If she enjoys fashion, encourage her to choose clothing that reflects her true selves and makes her smile happy. It's not about following trends; it's about finding ways to feel strong and true to yourself. There are many girls like different styles. Some like bold colors and patterns, while others like simple styles. Giving her the freedom to try on different styles teaches her that her clothes should represent who she is. This is not try to fit someone else's idea of beauty. I remember a family whose daughter loved putting together outfits with both old and upcoming clothes. She loved the process, and it helped her see how her body suits her style.

Art is another excellent way to show your personality. If she likes to draw, paint, or make things, tell her to produce items that show how unique she is. She could paint a picture of herself or draw a scene from her favorite place. She learns to value her own point of view and uniqueness by expressing herself through art. This helps her build a sense of identity that isn't based on how she looks.

Aside from music, dance, and writing, her hobbies also help her feel complete. She cares less about how she looks and more about what makes her feel good when doing something she loves. A mother I knew pushed her daughter to start taking pictures, which she loved doing. Her daughter started to notice the beauty in the world around her, and as a result, she came to see it in herself as well.

Audrey Hepburn said, "A woman's beauty is not in her face; her true beauty is in her soul." By encouraging your daughter to express herself, you're helping her focus on the joy and uniqueness she has within. This will help her build a body image that values creativity and individuality over conformity.

<u>Change and Introspection</u>

By showing her what her body can do, giving her positive role models, and pushing her to express herself, you're aiding her develop a healthy, self-accepting view of her body. Think about how these methods might help her. How can you help her be proud of her body? Who are some positive examples she can look up to? And what activities or ways of expressing herself might enhance her feel truly herself?

Now that you have these valuable tools, let's look at "How to Help Her Make and Keep Friends."

GETTING HER TO LIKE HER BODY IN A WAY THAT WORKS

Putting the focus on what her body can do instead of how it looks

In a world that constantly emphasizes appearances, encouraging your daughter to value her body for its strength, toughness, and skills can significantly boost her confidence. When she values her body for its strength, toughness, and skills, she is less likely to let what others think define her. You give her a sense of self-worth that extends beyond how she looks by focusing on what her body allows her to do.

To begin, let's celebrate what her body can do. Can she play her favorite sport, climb trees, or dance to her favorite song? Tell her that these things are signs of her special power. For example, if she enjoys swimming, highlight her strength and coordination between her arms and legs. Also, tell her how her lungs help her breathe deeply and stay stable. This method can encourage her to feel grateful for her body's abilities, seeing it as a wonderful tool that lets her do the things she loves.

A family I know sparked their daughter's interest in climbing and encouraged her appreciate her legs and lungs by carrying her up steep hills. They celebrated every hill they climbed and every mile they ran as an adventure that showcased her strength. Instead of how she looked, she became proud of her body for what it could do. This pride helped her have a positive relationship with her body that wasn't based on what others thought was beautiful.

You can help her focus on her abilities instead of her looks. You can tell her to think of her body as something that lets her explore, create, and experience life. To quote Olympian and body-positive activist Allyson Felix, "Strength is showing up and being brave enough to embrace the body you have." Helping your daughter see her body as a source of strength will teach her that her worth isn't just skin deep, but in the things her body makes possible.

We can combat media and peer pressure by utilizing positive role models.

The things that the media and her friends say about her can affect how she sees herself. TV, newspapers, and even movies often propagate a narrow and false idea of beauty. This can lead to feelings of inadequacy and self-worth. A strong way to support her body image is to help her deal with these pressures by presenting her to a variety of positive role models. She discovers that beauty transcends societal expectations when she encounters confident, strong women who prioritize authenticity over appearance.

You could put her in touch with sports, artists, scientists, or organizers who are proud of who they are. They focus on their interests instead of their looks. You could show her figures of body-positive people like Serena Williams, who sees her muscles as a source of strength, or Ashley Graham, a model and author who defies beauty standards by loving her body just the way it is. These women provide her with real-life examples of women valued for their skills, knowledge, and self-confidence, in addition to their physical appearance.

I know another mom who told her daughter to follow social media accounts that support health, body confidence, and accepting herself. They each picked an account that celebrates variety and shares stories of women of all shapes and sizes who are doing well. This helped her daughter see a wider range of beauty and understand that worth isn't based on how someone behaves over time. When she felt like she had to meet certain beauty standards, she would be reminded of the women she loved. She would also remember that confidence isn't just about looks.

Tell her to think about what she reads and hears in the media. Every time she sees an advertisement for a " Ideal " body, ask her, "Do you believe everyone looks like that?" What makes a person strong or beautiful besides how they appear? Teaching her to think critically gives her the tools to survive a world full of false perceptions. An organizer and founder of the "I Weigh" movement, Jameela

Jamil, says, "Your body is not your enemy; your body is your home." By showing her people who live by this truth, you help her see that there are many ways to be happy and feel positive about yourself.

Encourage individuals to express themselves through art, fashion, or hobbies.

A fun and powerful way to help your daughter feel positive about her body is to let her express herself. When she has fashion, art, or other hobbies that let her explore her personality, she values her uniqueness. She finds ways to express herself that inspire her to feel comfortable. Self-expression helps her become more comfortable in her own skin because it allows her to see her body as a blank surface for art instead of something to compare it to.

If she enjoys fashion, advise her to choose clothing that reflects her true self and makes her smile happy. It's not about following trends; it's about finding ways to feel strong and true to yourself. There are many girls who like different styles. Some like bold colors and patterns, while others like simple styles. Giving her the freedom to try on different styles teaches her that her clothes should be reflective of who she is. This is not try to fit someone else's idea of beauty. I remember a family whose daughter loved putting together outfits with both old and updated clothes. She loved the process, and it helped her see how her body suits her style.

Art is another excellent way to show your personality. If she likes to draw, paint, or make things, tell her to produce items that show how unique she is. She could paint a picture of herself or draw a scene from her favorite place. She learns to value her own point of view and uniqueness by expressing herself through art. This helps her build a sense of identity that isn't based on how she looks.

Aside from music, dance, and writing, her hobbies also help her feel complete. She cares less about how she looks and more about what makes her feel good when doing something she loves. A mother I knew pushed her daughter to start taking pictures, which she loved doing. Her daughter started to notice the beauty in the world around her, and as a result, she came to see it in herself as well.

Audrey Hepburn said, "A woman's beauty is not in her face; her true beauty is in her soul." By encouraging your daughter to express herself, you're helping her focus on the joy and uniqueness she has within. This will help her build a body image that values creativity and individuality over conformity.

<u>Change and Introspection</u>

By showing her what her body can do, giving her positive role models, and pushing her to express herself, you're encouraging her to develop a healthy, self-accepting view of her body. Think about how these methods might help her. How can you help her be proud of her body? Who are some positive examples she can look up to? And what activities or ways of expressing herself might enhance her feel truly herself?

Now that you have these handy tools, let's look at "How to Help Her Make and Keep Friends."

HOW CAN I HELP HER DEVELOP FRIENDSHIPS?

We strive to establish connections through common interests.

Getting to know friends is easier for many kids when they can talk about the things they both like. Finding people who like the same things as your daughter, whether she enjoys animals, reading, art, or science, can enable her to make friends. Shared interests not only help her feel like she fits in but also serve as a natural starting point for conversations and a chance to get to know each other better. You can help her find relaxed and real friends by focusing on the things they share.

Tell her to join clubs or groups where she can meet people who like the same things she does. A book club might be a wonderful place for her if she loves to read. If she likes sports, joining a neighborhood team might let her meet people who share her love of activity. The space itself becomes a welcoming place that helps people feel comfortable speaking to each other. She'll easily have things to talk about with her friends in art class, like her favorite artists or the latest projects she's worked on. This place lets her connect over a shared interest instead of pushing her to talk.

When my daughter loved animals, a mother I know helped her find a volunteer group at a nearby animal shelter. There, she met people who loved animals as much as she did. She felt at ease with them because they had something in common. She felt calm and at ease in this place, which made getting to know friends less daunting. Finding a group where she could be herself without feeling judged made a huge difference in her confidence.

When kids make friends through shared interests, they learn that relationships don't have to feel forced—they can just happen because of things they both love. "True belonging doesn't require you to change who you are; it requires you to be who you are," said Dr. Brené Brown. For her, making friends based on shared hobbies lets her be herself and creates bonds that keep her content and give her a sense of belonging.

She engages in social activities to enhance her sense of self-worth.

Sometimes it can be scary to connect with others, especially kids who don't easily pick up on social cues. By acting out these situations at home, she can gain the courage to talk to new people and venture into unfamiliar situations without worrying. By role-playing, she can experiment with various responses, enhance her communication skills, and acclimate to common social situations in a secure, stress-free environment.

You can begin by learning easy ways to say hello and greet someone. For example, she could play the role of the first friend she meets at school. She should practice saying, "Hello, my name is [name]." I really like what she's interested in. How about you? This gives her a starting point, so she doesn't have to think about how to start a talk. You can then move on to situations like joining a group exercise, responding yes to an offer, or being polite when disagreeing with someone. Each situation can be a chance for her to work through her worries and learn how to act in real life.

A family I knew did role-playing once a week to improve their daughter's social skills in a fun and helpful way. They would role-play situations, such as inviting a friend to join a game or extending a favor to a friend, and discuss the natural reactions that might occur. This practice enabled her to feel more comfortable around others and gave her the courage to talk to her friends. She felt like she had a support system, which made stepping out with others less scary.

She can also receive gentle advice without being criticised. Stop the situation in the middle to discuss other options or how others interpret different answers. This activity not only makes her smile better about herself, but also makes her more socially aware. "People will forget what you said, but they will never forget how you made them feel," Maya Angelou once said. Role-playing helps her be kind and supportive of herself, which helps her build positive memories with her friends.

She teaches empathy and emphasizes mutual respect in relationships.

Respect and understanding are at the heart of any lasting bond. You can help your daughter make deep relationships with others by teaching her to understand and respect their feelings. She can also expect the same in return. When both people in a friendship feel valued and understood, the friendship grows. When she learns to develop these traits in her relationships, she forms bonds that transcend beyond simple interactions.

It might be helpful to explain empathy in simple terms, such as "putting yourself in someone else's shoes." When she can think about how her friend might feel, she's more likely to be patient and kind. If a friend is having a difficult day, for example, tell her to think about how a small act, like giving her a kind word or sharing her favorite snack, could make a difference. Let her know that empathy doesn't always mean fixing someone's problem. Sometimes all she needs to do is listen and show she cares.

In real life, a family I know taught their daughter kindness by reading stories. They would talk about how the actors might feel in different situations after reading a story together. These talks helped her understand her feelings and practice thoughtful answers. She became known as someone who really listened and cared over time, as she used this understanding in her own friendships.

It's just as significant to teach her about respecting others. To show respect in a friendship, she needs to accept differences, listen without blaming over someone, and set healthy limits. Tell her it's okay to talk about how she feels about a friend being mean to her and, if necessary, take a step back. When people appreciate each other's feelings, she knows they are important. She can expect her friends to be kind to her just as she is kind to them.

"Kindness and patience are necessary for mutually caring relationships," Fred Rogers once said. When she learns to show these traits in her friendships, she builds bonds based on trust and support. These basics not only make her friendships stronger, but they also show her how to have relationships that will make her life better for years to come.

<u>Change and Introspection</u>

You're giving her the tools to make and keep significant bonds by encouraging friendships based on shared interests. She's practicing social skills through role-play, and learning empathy and mutual respect. Think about how these methods might be beneficial to her. What hobbies do you both have that could help you connect with others? How could role-playing situations enable her overcome social fears? What kind of acts of kindness and respect can help her form lasting friendships that bring her happiness?

So now that you have these basic skills, let's talk about "Teaching the Unwritten Rules of Social Life."

Teaching Social Rules That Aren't Written Down

Understanding social cues and body language simultaneously can be challenging.

Understanding social cues and body language can be like deciphering unspoken language. Many kids, especially those who struggle with social situations, may not always recognize these cues. Your daughter will feel more confident and handle social situations better if you help her read body language and other minor social cues. By talking over these cues with her, you can help her feel like she is planning how to communicate with others.

Start with simple things, like body language and facial movements. You could discuss each face's meaning as you look at the pictures. For example, a smile usually means someone is friendly or happy, while crossed arms could mean someone is protective or uncomfortable. It can even be enjoyable if you show her a picture of someone's face and ask, "What do you think that person is feeling?" This allows her to practice without the pressure of interacting with people in real time.

You could use real-life examples to show these signs. Let's say you're in the park and see someone who smiles at you and seems willing to talk. Discuss with her the possibility of initiating a conversation with someone with similar body language. Seeing these signs in everyday life can help her understand how others feel and know how comfortable they are with her.

You can also relate to these skills better if you have lived them yourself. Talk about times when you got a social cue wrong and what you learned from it. An expert on emotional intelligence, Dr. Daniel Goleman, says, "Emotional intelligence starts developing in the early years." Simple things kids say to their parents, teachers, and each other send significant messages. By discussing over these cues with her, you're building her emotional intelligence and making her feel better prepared for social situations.

You're helping her understand groups' functioning and navigating social advancement.

Unwritten hierarchies and shifting relationships within a group can create confusion. If you help your daughter deal with these issues, she may feel less nervous in social situations. You're giving her the power to handle social situations with more understanding and less stress. This is done by teaching her tools to spot patterns in group behavior.

Describe the concept of individual roles in groups, including how some individuals prefer to take the lead, others prefer to observe, and still others contribute in the background. Say the students are working on a project together at school. One might easily step up and plan, while others give ideas or do the work. Talk to her about the different roles people play and help her figure out where she feels most at ease. Remind her that every part is critical and contributes to the group succeed.

Playing a role can provide assistance with this. She should practice situations where she might encounter different personalities, such as engaging in a group discussion or responding when someone takes the lead. Consider the scenario where she joins a group of friends already engaged in conversation. She should first listen, wait for a natural pause, and then contribute her thoughts. This will help her learn how to join in. This practice can alleviate her nervousness by providing her with strategies to engage with the group without becoming overwhelmed.

A family I know taught their daughter about group dynamics by watching her favorite TV shows together. They watched how the characters interacted with each other. They would pause scenes to discuss why one character was in charge or why another kept quiet. This activity made her feel more at ease with group relationships in real life by giving her a fun and safe way to practice observing them.

Author of wisdom Stephen Covey recommended, "Prioritize understanding before seeking understanding." By teaching her to approach group dynamics with an open mind, you're showing her that understanding other people's roles can help her feel more at ease, which will help her find her place without forcing herself into a role that doesn't seem natural.

You should explain the concept of personal space and boundaries.

Personal space and limits are critical parts of social life. To build healthy, comfortable relationships, your daughter should understand, accept, and set her own limits. Personal space is more than just being away from someone physically. It also means being aware of when to give someone mental space and when to ask for it herself.

To describe personal space, use the term "social bubbles." Explain how everyone has a safety zone that is like an unseen bubble around them. Close family and friends may need a smaller space to hug or sit together. The circle is usually broader for people she knows but doesn't know very well. To work on this together, try standing close to each other and then stepping back to show how different levels of contact feel. This approach helps her gain a more concrete understanding of a concept that may initially seem ambiguous.

Make them understand that limits aren't just physical but also mental and verbal. Help her understand when someone doesn't want to talk about a certain subject. Also, when it's polite to say, "I don't feel like talking about that." Also, teach her to be aware of when she's becoming uncomfortable and to be clear about her own limits. She can say things like "I need some space right now" or "I'd rather talk about something else." By practicing these lines with her, you give her the words to protect her own safety.

A family engaged their daughter in a "comfort zone" game to teach her boundaries. It was each person's turn to talk about a situation and decide what felt right or wrong. "What would you think if someone stood really close to you in line?" "What would you do if a friend told you a secret that made you feel dragged?" This game taught her to pay attention to her feelings and choose what brings her joy.

"Daring to set boundaries is about loving ourselves, even when we risk disappointing others," says author and researcher Dr. Brené Brown. Teaching your daughter to respect and communicate boundaries will help her make friends who treat her with respect. This will make her friendships feel safe, comfortable, and real.

<u>Change and Introspection</u>

You're helping her figure out the often-unspoken rules of social life by reading her body language, knowing how groups work, and giving her space. Think about how these tools will help her. What signs does she already notice? How might watching people interact in a group make her feel better? What words or phrases can she use to tell you no?

Now that you have these aforementioned social tools, let's look at "A Step-by-Step Guide to Teaching Life Skills."

Chapter 4: Communication and Learning

*"The single biggest problem in communication is the illusion that it has taken place." –
George Bernard Shaw*

We support expression through speech and body language.

There are many ways to describe yourself, and for some kids, talking to others doesn't fully show how they feel or think. By encouraging your daughter to express herself through art, music, or writing, you give her more ways to say what she feels and thinks. These artistic activities are more than just hobbies for her; they're powerful tools that help her connect with others in a way that seems natural and satisfying.

You could give her a small area with paper, paint, pencils, or markers so she can draw or paint whenever she wants. Tell her that she can show how she feels or thinks through colors, shapes, and textures. For example, when she's energetic and energized, she might make a bright, swirling design. When she's thoughtful, she might paint a soft, calm landscape. She can talk without words through her art, which is a safe, judgment-free way to share her inner world.

Music is another wonderful way to show yourself. She can connect with and share her feelings through music, whether she likes to listen, sing, or even learn an instrument. She might be able to deal with her worries or stress better if she listens to a soothing song. She can also use joyful songs to celebrate if she's in the mood. Some parents even make "emotion playlists" with their kids, where they pick songs that fit different moods. This could be a fun and intriguing way for her to use music to connect with her feelings.

Writing is also a wonderful way to describe yourself. You could encourage her to maintain a journal where she can record about her day, express her emotions, or even create original songs and stories. My friend's family had their daughter keep a "gratitude journal" where she wrote down things she was thankful for every night. She connected with her feelings and said what she thought in a safe environment. The fact that she could write down how she felt helped her feel better over time.

Picasso once said, "Art washes away everyday life." By encouraging her to be artistic, you're helping her find more creative ways to talk about and work through her feelings, which will give her a sense of freedom and self-understanding that extends beyond words.

Teaching different ways to talk, like sign language or visual aids

Alternative ways of communicating can be life-changing for some kids, giving them creative ways to connect with others and express themselves. She can use tools like communication boards, sign language, or visual aids to talk to people in ways that feel easier or more natural to her than speaking. These aren't just "substitutes"; they're real ways for her to talk to people and connect with them.

If she is having trouble finding the right words, picture cards or message boards can be very helpful. For example, if she has trouble putting her feelings into words, she could use cards with different faces that show different emotions (happy, unhappy, angry, etc.) to express how she's feeling. You could also give her a simple board with choices to help her figure out what she wants. For her, visual tools make it easier to talk about her wants and needs by giving her an organized way to do so.

Another useful skill is sign language. She might have trouble talking, but showing her some simple signs, like "please," "yes," "help," and "no," can make a big difference in how she interacts with others. You don't have to learn a whole language at once. Begin by choosing a few everyday words. Families discover that signing a few words while conversing enhances the quality of the conversation by establishing a connection between spoken words and visual cues.

People I know teach their daughters sign language by using simple signs in regular conversations. For example, "eat" before meals or "play" when it was time to play. Over time, she used these signs to communicate when words were challenging for her. It provided her with the freedom to communicate with others in a way that brought her joy, fostering a closer bond with her family and friends.

Helen Keller, who faced major communication problems, once said, "Blindness cuts us off from things, but deafness cuts us off from people." By showing her creative ways to speak, you're bridging that gap and giving her new tools to connect and talk with confidence.

Seeing and appreciating her unique communication style

Each one of them has their own way of talking, whether it's through words, smiles, or body language. Your daughter learns that there is no "right" or "wrong" way to communicate when you value and recognize her individual style. When you respect her unique style, you show her that her voice is important. This boosts her confidence and makes her feel like you understand her.

Look at how confidently she talks about herself. How does she express her emotions? Does she use her face or her body? It's possible that she feels safer writing down her ideas than speaking them out loud. Pay attention to these small things and let her know you like her style. If she would rather nod or shake her head than say "yes" or "no," for example, accept that as an acceptable answer. Small things like this show her that you understand how she likes to talk to people.

You can also copy her look and make it your own. Show that you understand her by using the same body language or facial movements she does when talking. I once knew a mother whose daughter communicated through drawing. She wouldn't force her to " speak " about her day; instead, she would draw with her and ask her questions about them. This method helped her daughter feel seen and understood without having to say what she was thinking.

She can see that the conversation isn't about being a perfectionist as long as she values her own way. Maya Angelou once said, "People will forget what you said, but they will never forget how you made them feel." By respecting her unique way of talking, you support her sense that her voice is meaningful, no matter what form it takes.

<u>Change and Introspection</u>

You give her the tools to express herself with confidence and honesty. This is done by encouraging artistic outlets, teaching her more creative ways to communicate, and recognizing her unique style. Think about how these methods could help her. What creative activities do you know she enjoys? How would you feel about using a different way of talking? And what can you do to show her that her unique way of talking is okay and appreciated?

Now that she has these ways to describe herself, let's talk about teaching her to advocate for herself with confidence."

I AM TEACHING HER HOW TO CONFIDENTLY SPEAK UP FOR HERSELF.

Assist her in identifying her needs and articulating them effectively.

A basic skill for self-advocacy is teaching your girl how to figure out what she wants and say what she wants. She will be able to handle social situations, school, and other places with more confidence. This is once she knows what she needs to feel safe, supported, and at ease. By aiding her in articulating her needs with clarity and confidence, you empower her to contribute to a world that values her uniqueness.

Start by telling her to think about how she feels. Simply asking her questions such as "What calms you down?" or "What do you require when you have too much to do?" can help her identify her needs. Asking simple questions such as "What calms you down?" or "What do you need when you have too much to do?" can help her identify her needs. You could even make a list together, including things like physical comfort (sound, lights), social comfort (alone time, time with friends), and learning style (visual tools, quiet places). This process isn't about fixing her pain; it's about giving her words to describe it. She's already speaking up for herself when she describes what she wants.

A mother I worked with kept a "needs journal" for her daughter. It was a small notebook where her daughter could write down things that made her feel better. From taking short breaks during homework to asking for quiet time after school, her daughter discovered over time what worked best for her. She learned more about herself through this activity, and now she feels confident enough to ask others for these changes.

Help her learn phrases like "I need some alone time" or "It would be better if we could do this in a quieter area." When she practices these phrases, she will understand that requesting for what she wants is not a sign of weakness but of self-awareness and respect. Louise Hay, a self-help author, once asserted, "You possess the power to transform your life, and it's crucial to understand this." Teaching her to state her needs gives her the power to change her surroundings in ways that benefit her health.

She can improve her assertiveness by engaging in advocacy scenarios.

Having her play different roles can help her feel more comfortable speaking up for herself. By practicing different speaking situations in a safe space, she improves her confidence when speaking. Real-life events can be challenging to handle, but you can help her get ready for them by practicing things like asking for help in class, setting limits with friends, and saying what she wants.

Start with the simple things that happen every day. Suppose she needs more time on a test or would rather be in a quieter area of the classroom. You could act out a situation like this. Take turns teaching and learning to improve her speaking and listening. She can find words that feel normal to her by trying different ones. This will help her remember them in real life. Saying things like "May I please sit somewhere quiet?" or "Could we have more time to work on this?" will strengthen her ability to speak up for herself in a cool and confident way. These actions strengthen her ability to speak up for herself coolly and confidently.

A family I know helped their daughter learn how to connect with others by role-playing. They practiced times when she might want to say what she wanted. For example, picking out a game to play with friends or asking for a break when she was too busy. By practicing, she improved her ability to advocate for herself, as she understood the appropriate responses in various situations. This practice gave her the courage to tell her friends what she needed, which made social situations less scary.

Talk about how she felt after each role-play. Ask, "What was easy about that?" or "What made you feel horrible?" She can learn from the experience and change what didn't work by thinking about it again. "You must do the things you think you can't do," Eleanor Roosevelt said. By practicing speaking in low-stress settings, you're giving her more confidence to face these challenges and reaffirming that she can handle tough situations and explain clearly.

Assisting her in realizing the importance of her voice could be the most crucial aspect of teaching her self-advocacy skills. Telling her that her thoughts, feelings, and wants are important will boost her self-esteem and inspire her to speak up. When you value her opinion, she will advocate for herself. Holding onto this idea will demonstrate to her that she is deserving of kindness and respect.

Start by showing her that you value her opinion in your everyday conversations. Listen carefully and think about what to say when she shares her thoughts or needs. Tell her you respect her point of view, even if you don't always agree with it. For example, if she says that a certain job is too much for her, let her know that you understand by saying, "I hear that this is hard for you." She discovers the power of her voice and its ability to influence her environment when she feels heard.

Make it a safe place for her to say what she's feeling and thinking by encouraging her to do so often. One mom I knew set aside ten minutes every night for "talking time" with her daughter, where they'd talk about anything that was on her mind. This developed into a cherished custom, providing her daughter with a consistent opportunity to express herself without fear of judgment. Her daughter got the courage to speak her mind by doing this, which set her up for future success in advocating for herself.

Keep telling her that her wants and needs are important and that she can say what she wants. It's painful to carry an unwritten story inside you, as Maya Angelou once said. Reminding her that her voice should be heard helps her see that speaking up for herself is not only okay but necessary. This idea turns into a strong weapon she can carry with her, giving her the confidence to be herself in every part of her life.

<u>Change and Introspection</u>

By helping her identify her needs, practicing advocacy scenarios, and reminding her of the importance of her voice, you equip her with the tools she needs to be her own champion with confidence and kindness. Think about how these methods might help her grow. What specific needs does she feel comfortable discussing? How could role-playing help her advocate better for herself? What regular messages can give her know her voice matters?

Now that you know how to advocate for others, let's explore "Why Learning Can Be Hard for Autistic Girls—and How to Help."

Understand Why Autistic Girls Struggle to Learn and How to Help.

Understanding how sensory challenges impact learning is crucial.

For girls with autism, learning isn't just about getting updated information; it's also about controlling their senses. The sensory world of a normal classroom can be very stressful for people with sensory problems. Bright lights, loud noises, and even the feel of some materials make it difficult for her to focus on one thing at a time. You can understand how these problems affect her ability to learn and think clearly once you know them.

Think about a classroom with bright lights and noise all the time. Some kids don't notice these things, but autistic kids find them upsetting. The hum of the lights might be too loud to bear, or the talk of peers might mix together into a cacophony that makes it difficult to concentrate. Not only do these physical experiences affect her mood, they can also make it challenging for her to understand what's going on around her. Every time she has to mentally block out a physical trigger, it takes mental energy away from learning, causing her exhausted and worried.

A mother I know noticed that her daughter had trouble focusing on her homework because of all the different sounds and sights at school. Together with her daughter, she created a sensory-friendly study area at home, incorporating soft lighting, noise-canceling headphones, and a weighted lap pad. After lowering sensory overload, her daughter was able to focus better and finish her work with less worry. By being aware of these physical needs at home, she was able to push for similar help at school, which made a huge difference in her daughter's comfort and success.

Temple Grandin, a famous autistic champion, once said, "I am different, not less." Understanding how sensory issues affect learning helps her feel better about her situation and tells her that it's okay to need a different place to learn. Understanding and meeting these emotional needs can make her school experience better, giving her a safe place to learn, grow, and focus without always feeling overloaded.

They adapt their teaching methods to better align with her learning style.

Every child learns differently, and for autistic girls, adapting your teaching methods to suit their learning style can have a significant difference. Traditional ways of teaching might not always work for her, so making the information fit the way she thinks can help her feel more involved and capable. She can learn best by seeing things, doing them, or repeating them over and over again. Making lessons fit her learning style teaches her that learning doesn't have to be difficult; it can be fun.

First, pay attention to her hobbies. As an example, if she likes drawing, tell her to use mind maps or color-coded notes to assist her remember things. Hands-on tasks can help her understand complex ideas if she's interested in building things. For instance, when she studies math, demonstrate various shapes using building blocks. This method helps her understand and remember the knowledge in a way that feels natural by connecting the idea to something real.

A family I worked with found that their girl learned best by listening to stories. Instead of doing regular math questions, they used the math to make up stories, adding people and situations to each one. They turned math from a stressful subject into a fun and intriguing one by making the lessons fit her hobbies. This method not only aided her in learning but also bolstered her confidence, as she felt understood and encouraged.

"It's not how smart you are; it's how you are smart," says Dr. Howard Gardner, famous for his theory of multiple intelligences. When you change the way you teach to fit her unique learning style, you build her confidence and reinforce her skills. It's less about fitting into a mold and more about finding her own way to success as she learns.

Building a friendship with school staff and teachers is crucial.

For your girl to do well at school, she needs a positive bond with her teachers and other staff. When teachers know what she needs and work with you, they form a team committed to her success. By getting to know her, you're ensuring she has a group of people who see her strengths, deal with her problems, and help her grow.

First, have an honest talk with her teachers about how she learns best. Discuss any sensory needs she has, and any changes that make her feel more at ease. Emphasize that optimal learning occurs when specific factors are considered, such as providing her with additional time for tasks, providing a quiet environment for tests, or providing visual aids. The point isn't to get "special treatment," but to make sure she has a suitable place to learn where she can do well. Most teachers like these ideas and are eager to find ways to help their students.

One mom I know met with her daughter's teachers on a daily basis to talk about growth and problems. They even created a shared "communication notebook" for use both at home and at school. The teacher would write in it about her day and any problems she had. Because they could communicate, the mother and teacher could make small changes when needed. This team-based method helped her daughter feel understood and supported at school, which made her less anxious and helped her concentrate better.

Remind your daughter that her teachers are there for her and will help her. Encourage her to tell them what she needs when she is ready. Tell her that speaking up at school helps her and that her teachers want to help her succeed. Helen Keller, a person who had a lot of trouble learning, once said, "Alone we can do so little; together we can do so much." Building a relationship of support with school staff shows her that her education is a team effort and that people believe in her potential.

Change and Introspection

You're making a learning space that values her unique needs and strengths by understanding her sensory challenges, changing your teaching methods, and getting to know the school staff on a personal level. As you help her on her journey, think about these ideas: What changes to her senses could make learning more comfortable? How could personalized ways of training help her reach her full potential? What steps can you take to ensure that you can easily communicate with her teachers, enabling you to support her at all times?

Let's discuss "Using Her Special Interests to Unlock Success" now that we have established these fundamentals.

She combines her distinct interests to achieve her goals.

She leverages her interests to enhance her academic performance and her daily life.

A wonderful way to make your daughter do well is to use her hobbies to learn critical life and school skills. When she finds interest in her activities, she naturally learns. Special interests are often more than just hobbies; they can bring you joy, assist you concentrate, or even unwind. Making these interests into educational opportunities will not only make school more fun, but also help her feel more confident in a way that feels very personal.

First, look for ways to connect her interests to things she is learning at school. For instance, if she has a fondness for animals, you could leverage her interest in biology by exploring their behavior and habitats. Imagine how excited she will be to learn about different landscapes or the bodies of animals through things that interest her already. She can approach schoolwork this way because it makes her interested and excited about learning. She may even become so engrossed in the subject that she explores it beyond school hours by watching programs or reading books about it.

I worked with a family whose girl loved the stars. They didn't separate her interest from her studies; instead, they used her love of the stars to teach her math concepts by having her figure out how far objects are in space and science concepts by showing her how stars die and come back to life. This merging not only helped her do well in school, but it also helped her understand things that were challenging for her at first. They demonstrated to her how her hobbies could lead to the acquisition of new skills and knowledge by engaging her in topics she was passionate about.

Albert Einstein once said, "It is the supreme art of the teacher to awaken joy in creative expression and knowledge." By using her hobbies as a starting point, you can turn learning into something she looks forward to instead of something she has to go through. This excitement not only helps her do better in school, but it also makes her love learning that goes beyond the classroom.

People can learn new things through their hobbies.

Hobbies can be very motivating, helping you get out of your comfort zone and try out various, difficult ideas. She can learn in a way that is enjoyable and simple for her when you base it on her interests. She is ready to try various things because she is passionate about them, even if they are outside her comfort zone. It's smart to use her interests as a starting point. This is so she can discover more about new things by connecting them to something she already likes and knows.

For instance, if she really loves art, you could use it to help her learn about math ideas like patterns, symmetry, or ratios. She could enjoy learning about proportions through face drawing or exploring math applications in building plans. The visual link between her hobby and the idea gives her something to connect vague ideas to. This makes them easier to understand and less scary.

A mother engaged in this activity with her daughter, who loved cooking. She used recipes to teach simple science, fractions, and measurement. They would rather bake together than do math problems. As they progressed, they would measure items and talk about ratios. The "math lessons" her daughter loved didn't feel like school; they felt like fun cooking classes. Because of this, my daughter felt better about her math skills and was excited to learn without even understanding it.

"Flow" psychologist Mihaly Csikszentmihalyi once said, "The best times in our lives are not the passive, receptive, relaxing times... but the moments when we are fully engaged." By relating learning to her hobbies, you're creating these engaged moments, making new ideas feel simple to understand and fun, and giving her a sense of accomplishment.

> **She should take pride in her achievements in her passions.**

Celebrating her successes, particularly those that align with her hobbies, can significantly boost her confidence. Recognizing and respecting her skills motivates her to grow. Recognizing her success in the things she loves makes her feel like her interests are important. This can be especially motivating if she's had trouble in standard school situations. By praising her efforts, you show her that being successful isn't just about getting excellent grades or doing what everyone else does; it's also about developing the things that make her special.

Find meaningful ways to praise her growth. If she loves music, take her to a concert in your area to show your support for her efforts to learn an instrument. If she really enjoys reading, plan a party where she can share a favorite book that she has finished. These celebrations don't need to be extravagant; the key thing is to acknowledge them. By focusing the party on her interests, you demonstrate your recognition of her passions.

One girl from a family I knew had a deep love for animals and aspired to work with them. In her animal science club, they celebrated her every accomplishment, such as learning how to care for pets or naming various animal breeds. They took her to a nearby zoo or wildlife area every time she met a new goal so she could use what she had learned in the real world. This kind of gathering made her more dedicated to her interest and showed her that it was worth more than just schooling.

Fred Rogers said it so well: "We all have different gifts, so we all have different ways of telling the world who we are." Celebrating her successes in the things she loves gives her a proud way to show off her unique gifts. It teaches her that being successful doesn't just mean following the rules; it also means accepting what makes her unique. These events help her feel positive about who she is and show her that she can be outstanding in her own way.

<u>Change and Introspection</u>

You can help her achieve success on her own terms by combining her interests with schoolwork. You can also use her hobbies to keep her motivated to succeed, and praising her successes in things she enjoys. Think about how these methods can give her more power. Which of her hobbies could help her learn? How can her interests make learning new things more fun? And how might recognizing her unique accomplishments improve her feel better about herself?

Now that you have these effective methods, let's look at "Easy Tips for Time Management and Organization."

SHE'S SLOWING DOWN AT HER OWN PACE.

Establishing realistic objectives that align with her distinct abilities is crucial.

Each child grows at a different rate, so it's critical to establish goals for your girl based on her specific skills and strengths. She builds her self-confidence by setting goals she can reach. This helps her feel strong instead of stressed. She should be able to reach her goals, giving her something to work toward without feeling stressed. You're giving her a clear path to success that seems both meaningful and doable by setting these goals that fit her specific skills.

Begin by setting small, clear goals that align with her hobbies or skills. If she likes art, her first goal could be to draw something simple every week. Someone who likes to cook might aim to make their own food. These types of goals enable her to enhance her existing skills, increase her self-esteem, and encourage her to explore new experiences. She feels better about herself when she meets a small, clear goal. This can motivate her to take on higher-level tasks in the future.

One family I worked with gave their daughter weekly goals based on how much she loved being outside. They told her that every week she should learn the names of one or two plants. This small step fit with her hobbies and seemed doable. It also helped her learn new things in a fun and satisfying way. Starting with something she liked gave her a sense of progress, which motivated her to find out more. Over time, she assigned herself tasks, such as naming plants while hiking with her family.

If her goals align with her skills and hobbies, she will be more driven and less likely to give up. "The good life is a process, not a state of being," said psychologist

Carl Rogers. It's a way to get somewhere. By giving her goals that are attainable, you're showing her the way and letting her grow at her own pace, with joy and confidence.

Recognizing even the smallest successes can inspire your daughter to keep striving, as growth is not always linear. She can see that growth is a journey full of small wins when she notices her progress, no matter how small. Celebrating her dedication to work sends her a message of appreciation, which strengthens her and keeps her inspired.

Set up habits to track her growth. These could be something as simple as a thank-you note, a sticker on the wall, or a high-five for a job well done. She needs to know that every action, like finishing a difficult school task, trying something challenging, or just working hard every day, counts. Honor the seemingly insignificant things she does, like putting her toys away or making her bed, as she learns to keep her room clean. These times of praise don't just show her appreciation; they also let her know that you see how hard she's working, which reinforces how significant it is to keep pushing forward.

A family I knew kept a "success jar" for their daughter. They would write her goal down on a piece of paper and put it in the jar every time she reached it, no matter how small. At the end of each month, they read all the notes and were proud of their small accomplishments. This became a special family tradition that made her remember how much she had grown and encouraged her to keep trying. Seeing real proof of her progress gave her confidence and taught her that every step forward, no matter how modest, was something to be proud of.

"Enthusiasm is common," says Dr. Angela Duckworth, who is known for her work on grit. "Endurance is rare." Teaching her to enjoy small wins will help her build endurance to keep going. By focusing on her progress instead of perfection, you're making her see that every effort contributes to her grow. This will help her develop an attitude that values strength and consistency.

Maintaining a balance between support and independence is crucial for growth. Giving your daughter gentle advice shows her that you're there to help her, not tell her what to do all the time. Your freedom to choose and learn from her own mistakes will help her take responsibility for her own growth. This method shows her that you believe in her skills, which boosts her confidence as she faces difficult obstacles.

If she is having trouble with a job, assist her by demonstrating to her how to do it instead of doing it for her. For instance, you could demonstrate how to make her a bed without doing it for her. Let her try one step at a time, and give her support as she progresses. Putting her through small challenges helps her grow. If something happens wrong, reassure her without jumping in immediately. You could say, "I know this is a challenge, but you're doing great." "Let's figure it out together" communicates your belief in her ability to overcome challenging situations.

A mother I know told her daughter to do a few things around the house, like setting the table for dinner. When her daughter was initially hesitant, she assisted her and provided gentle guidance. Her daughter became more self-confident over time and started setting the table by herself. She became independent at her own pace because her mom was always there to guide her if she needed it.

As Fred Rogers reportedly said, "Life doesn't give you time for everything you want, so you have to choose." Your choices should be based on a deep understanding of who you are. By giving her gentle advice without being too pushy, you're helping her make true decisions. This method helps her become more independent by showing her that she can grow at her own pace and in her own way.

<u>Change and Introspection</u>

You can help her grow in a way that respects her unique pace and skills. This is done by giving her gentle advice, setting attainable goals, and praising her progress. Consider how these strategies can empower her: what achievable small goals could boost her confidence? How can you make traditions to honor her progress? What kind of gentle advice could help her become independent?

Now that we have established these caring foundations, let's delve into "Supporting Verbal and Non-Verbal Expression."

How to Help Her Do It on Her Own

We teach everyday life skills through hands-on practice.

Teaching everyday life skills is the first step toward freedom, but the most effective way to learn them is to do it yourself. Life skills are more than just school skills; they provide her the confidence to face the world and the ability to do daily chores by herself. When you teach her skills like cooking, cleaning, and personal hygiene by doing them yourself, you provide her with the tools to be independent. You also give her a sense of accomplishment.

First, give her easy, age-appropriate jobs that will help her feel positive about herself. For example, if she loves food, consider involving her in simple kitchen tasks such as washing vegetables or measuring out ingredients. As she becomes accustomed to them, introduce various tasks such as stirring or seasoning. Keep doing this until she is comfortable enough to make a simple meal on her own with your help. With each step she completes successfully, she learns to take care of things on her own.

As a way to teach their daughter life skills, one family I worked with made a "morning routine checklist." They practiced each step, like brushing her teeth, getting dressed, and making the bed, together until it became second nature to her. This step-by-step method helped her learn various skills without getting too stressed, which reassured her that she could become independent. She became proud of taking charge of her morning routine over time because she knew she could do it on her own.

Don't forget that each life skill she learns makes her more independent. "Never help a child with a task he feels he can succeed at," said Dr. Maria Montessori, the founder of the Montessori method. By letting her take care of her life skills, you show her that she can handle her world on her own, one small task at a time.

Encourage decision-making and problem-solving skills.

Making decisions and handling problems are key skills for independence. Encouraging her to practice these skills helps her trust her own judgment. She feels more at ease discovering her tastes and taking responsibility for her choices when she learns to come up with decisions on her own. The goal is not to keep her from making mistakes but to help her deal with minor problems. This is so she can learn how to fix them on her own.

Introduce her to daily choices, even small ones. Let her choose clothes, books, and after-school activities. Each option gives her a small taste of freedom and a chance to think carefully about what she wants. As she becomes accustomed to making decisions, the complexity of them increases. For example, let her decide how to spend her pay or plan a family activity. By doing this over and over, she builds a system for making decisions that she can depend on.

Help her figure out how to solve problems when they come up instead of fixing them right away. If she's having trouble with a school job, tell her to think of ways to finish it. To simplify the task, ask her, "What do you think would make this easier?" or "What could you do next?" By encouraging her to consider her options, you're demonstrating to her that patience and creativity can solve problems.

I knew a family whose daughter made a "decision journal." She wrote down a choice she made and how it turned out every week. Going over these options with you helped her understand how her choices affected things and gave her a chance to think about what worked and what didn't. Over time, she developed greater trust in her own intuition, feeling empowered to make decisions with confidence.

No matter what you do, you will face attacks, so follow your intuition. Encouraging her to make choices, even small ones, helps her learn to trust her gut and listen to her inner voice.

These skills will help her find her way as she becomes more independent.

These skills will provide her with a safety net while allowing her to take small risks.

Independence doesn't mean she's on her own all the time; it means offering her a safety net so she can explore, knowing she can get help if she needs it. It's imperative to take small steps to build grit and self-confidence, but as a parent, it's normal to wish to keep your child protected. By giving her a safe place to try small chances, you give her the power to learn, grow, and feel confident in her skills. This is while knowing she's not alone.

Find small risks she can safely take that are right for her age. For example, if she wants to walk to a friend's house nearby, you could go with her the first few times. Then, you could let her try it on her own as she gets stronger. Also, if she wants to try something new, tell her she can stop if she feels uncomfortable and encourage her to take the first steps, even if they are outside of her comfort zone. She learns that she can handle new situations with these small risks. If something goes wrong, she has the tools and help to deal with it.

One family I worked with set up "exploration days" for their daughter every month. On these days, they would engage in activities she had never done before, such as visiting a new park, or they would attempt something more daring, such as a new sport. Because her family was there for her, she felt safe enough to try things that scared her at first. She gained confidence as she learned that trying new things could be safe and fun by doing them little by little.

Talk about what went well and what she learned after each risk. She learned from her mistakes and grew from them by thinking about them. This helps her remember that getting out of her comfort zone is a beneficial thing. "Resilience is the ability to bounce back from adversity, frustration, and misfortune," said Dr. Edith Grotberg, a psychologist and expert on resilience. By letting her take small risks in a safe space, you teach her to face problems with confidence and resilience.

<u>Change and Introspection</u>

You're helping her become independent in a way that fits her pace and abilities. This is done by giving her chances to make choices, teaching her life skills through hands-on practice, and creating a safe space for small risks. Think about these methods. What skills can you use each other? How can you get her to make more choices every day? What safe and manageable risks could inspire her to venture into less familiar areas?

Now that you have these tools for freedom, let's talk about "recognizing danger without turning her afraid."

Chapter 5: Safety, Sexuality, and Building Connection

"Boundaries are a part of self-care. They are healthy, normal, and necessary." – Doreen Virtue

How to Help Her Do It on Her Own

Roleplaying to teach situational awareness

Being aware of your surroundings is a necessary skill for independence, but it can be challenging to teach generally. Role-playing makes this skill real and simple to use, and it gives her a chance to practice noticing her surroundings and acting in different situations. By assuming various roles, you provide her with a secure environment to experiment with various scenarios. You enhance her self-esteem, and teach her how to remain vigilant without succumbing to stress.

Start by thinking of simple things she might do every day. For example, crossing a busy street, moving through a crowded area, or figuring out if someone is following her in a store. Start each scenario by telling her about the place and asking her to name anything interesting or important she saw. As an example, when she needs to cross the street, tell her to look for things like traffic lights, parked cars, and other people walking. She can practice responding by waiting for the light to change, looking both ways, or asking for help if she's unsure of what to do. Each situation shows her that being aware of what's going on around her makes her make smart choices.

One mother I know helped her daughter learn situational awareness by acting out different social situations. For example, what should you do if a stranger asks for help finding something? They would exchange roles and discuss appropriate responses, such as directing the individual to speak with a staff member. In addition, they would advise her not to approach strangers. These practice sessions helped her daughter learn how to handle unexpected events gently, which prepared her to handle them alone in real life.

Tell her to use this knowledge in real life, like keeping track of exits in unfamiliar place or noticing sites on the way to a friend's house. The famous explorer Bear Grylls sums up survival in three words: never give up. Situational awareness means teaching her to notice, evaluate, and trust her ability to safely manage her surroundings. This will give her the tools to be independent without fear.

Finding safe adults and reliable places to get help is crucial.

Knowing who to talk to when you don't know what to do helps. Teaching her how to find trusted people and places gives her a sense of safety and lets her know she has help when she needs it. By letting her know about safe people and places, you're showing her that being independent doesn't mean being alone; it means knowing where to get help when she needs it.

First, talk about the kinds of people who can help, like teachers, store workers, police officers, or neighbors. Make it clear that safe adults are people who are in charge or who have a specific job to do, like a library or crossing guard. Talk about times when she might need help, like if she gets lost, gets split from you in a public place, or feels uneasy around someone she doesn't know. You can tell these people are safe because they wear outfits or name tags. Remind her that it's okay to ask for help.

A family I worked with and their daughter made a map of "safe places." They marked on a map places in their neighborhood where she could go for help, like a neighbor's house, the library, or a store close by. They visited these places, said hello to the locals, and discussed how to help her. She felt safer and more independent when she knew she had a network of places and people she could trust. She felt like she could confidently get around her neighborhood.

Remind them that asking for help is not a sign of failing but of making a beneficial choice. This lesson teaches her that being independent means knowing when to ask for help. Maya Angelou once said, "Alone, all alone; nobody, but nobody, can make it out here alone." By helping her build a network of people and places she can trust, you teach her that being strong means knowing when and how to ask for help.

Giving clear examples to explain the difference between safe and dangerous behavior

She must understand the distinction between safe and dangerous behavior in order to become independent. Giving her clear examples helps her figure out how to evaluate situations, spot possible red flags, and decide when to back off or ask for help. Giving her specific, real-life examples helps her figure out what feels right and what doesn't, giving her the power to make choices based on her knowledge and gut feelings.

Explain that safe actions are those that respect her comfort, space, and limits. As an example, a teacher giving a high-five or a friend asking before taking something from her would be safe. On the other hand, someone asking her to keep a secret from her parents or trying to lead her somewhere alone could be dangerous. Giving her specific examples helps her figure out what to do instead of general directions like "trust your gut."

A family I knew taught their daughter about safety by acting out different situations, like what to do if an adult asks her to get in the car or if a stranger comes up to her on the field. They discussed clear actions she could take, such as saying "No, thank you," approaching a trusted adult, or calling a parent. Her daughter learned how to spot and deal with dangerous situations by seeing these examples. This gave her the confidence to say no and set limits.

Remind her that no one has the right to make her feel dangerous or nervous and tell her to speak up if she feels that way. Make it clear to her that she can leave a setting that doesn't feel right, whether that means turning down a small request or leaving a bigger commitment. Scientist Dr. Henry Cloud, who is known for his work on limits, has said, "Boundaries make us who we are." Teaching her these limits gives her the tools to keep herself safe and confident in her freedom.

Change and Introspection

You're giving her important independence skills by teaching her to be aware of her surroundings. You're teaching her to find trusted people and trusted places, and tell the difference between safe and unsafe behaviors. Think about how these techniques can help her: what situations could benefit from role-playing? How can she practice finding places and people she trusts? What clear examples of limits can help her tell the difference between safe settings and unsafe settings?

So now that you have these basic skills, let's look at "Explaining Consent and Boundaries Clearly."

MAKING IT EASY TO UNDERSTAND CONSENT AND LIMITS

We use straightforward language to establish personal space and physical boundaries.

Your daughter will better understand agreement after learning about personal space and physical limits. Understanding personal space and its importance empowers her to establish her own boundaries and respect others'. Explain that personal space is everyone's "bubble" in simple terms. Some people prefer to stand close to others, while others prefer to be farther away.

You can start by using these ideas around the house. It can be enjoyable to alternately move closer and farther apart while asking each other, "Is this okay?" Or, "Is this too close?" This simple game teaches her that everyone is different when it comes to comfort and that it's okay and polite to check in with others. Remind her that she decides who can touch her and that she is free to say something if something makes her feel uncomfortable.

A family I knew piqued their daughter's interest in this concept by creating a game known as "bubble zone." They marked each family member's "bubble" with tape. They practiced asking each other for permission before entering into each other's space. This fun game helped their daughter understand personal space in a normal way. It made limits real and enjoyable.

Help her understand that different people have different privacy needs. For instance, she might be okay with hugging a close friend but prefer a high-five. "Daring to set boundaries is about having the courage to love ourselves, even when we risk disappointing others," said Dr. Brené Brown, a researcher known for her work on vulnerability and boundaries. Teaching her this early on will make her feel like her comfort matters and she controls her space.

I help her express "no" with grace and assurance.

Your girl can gain a powerful skill by saying "no" with confidence. It's not rude to tell her "no." It's about accepting her right to choose what's okay with her and knowing her boundaries. Teaching her to use "no" as a powerful yet gentle statement affirms her autonomy and the importance of respecting her limits.

Start by enacting various scenarios in which she might have to say "no." For instance, a friend might ask her to take something important, or someone might ask her to do something she doesn't want to do. Tell her to say "no" in a cool, clear voice and look the other person in the eyes if it makes her feel better. Keep telling her that she doesn't have to say too much; a simple "No, thank you" or "I'd rather not" will do. She learns that her "no" is an acceptable response by practicing this skill, which also makes it easier for her to stand up for herself without feeling negative about it.

There was a mom I knew who helped her daughter learn how to say "no" by giving her choices. They would practice saying "no" to things like sharing a favorite toy or politely turning down an offer. For her daughter, this helped her understand that saying "no" didn't mean she was mean; it meant she respected her comfort level. She learned over and over again that it was okay to set limits, even with people she liked and trusted.

Oprah Winfrey often said, "You only have to say yes to the things that bring you joy." Knowing that she has the ability to say "no" when necessary enhances her self-esteem. Teaching her that saying "no" is beneficial and not detrimental gives her the courage to stand up for herself in a way that is polite and feels normal.

We illustrate consent's significance through practical examples.

Her personal experience shows her that consent is more than permission—it's about respect. Asking for and giving permission easily and without pressure is consent. Once she knows this, she can easily give or refuse consent in any situation. This will help her feel more in control of her body and comfort.

Start by providing her with examples she already knows. Say something like, "Let's suppose you want to borrow a friend's book." You would ask first, right? You would accept her choice if she said "no." This straightforward example demonstrates the exchange of consent and the unquestionable respect for "no" as a complete response. Make it clear that everyone can say "no," and respecting others' limits is as imperative as her own.

Talk about school or social events too. For instance, if someone asks for a hug, tell her that it's okay to tell her "No, that's not okay with me" or give something else, like a high-five. Teaching her this concept helps her feel in charge while learning how to be kind and clear in social situations. Talking about different events helps her remember that permission is a general rule she can use all her life.

In their home, a family I knew always sought permission before hugging or touching someone's belongings. This showed their daughter that asking permission is a necessity, even when it comes to close family members. Over time, she got better at asking for permission herself, which made the family a place where everyone felt valued.

"Boundaries are the distance at which I can love you and me simultaneously," said Dr. Gabor Maté, a specialist in trauma and childhood development. Teaching her to set and respect boundaries through real-life situations gives her a balanced and respectful understanding of consent that she can apply to all of her relationships.

<u>Change and Introspection</u>

You're teaching her to respect herself and others by giving her personal space, teaching her how to say "no," and letting her practice real-life consent situations. Think about how these skills can help her: what models can help her understand personal space? How could role-playing help her feel more comfortable saying "no"? What examples from real life show how imperative permission is?

Now that you have acquired these crucial skills for respect and freedom, let's discuss "Talking About Romance, Gender, and Identity" together.

WE DISCUSS LOVE, GENDER, AND AUTHENTICITY.

Setting up a safe place where people can talk freely about their feelings

Knowing how you feel about love, gender, and identity is difficult. Making her feel supported by giving her a safe place to talk about her feelings is the first step. When she knows she can speak to you about anything, she learns that her feelings are okay, even if they seem strange or challenging to understand. She feels secure in the knowledge that you're being honest, and she doesn't have to deal with these things alone.

Start by being open with her when talking to her. Tell her that it's normal to feel any way she does, whether it's nervous, confused, or uncertain. Don't give advice or draw conclusions immediately. Instead, listen to her and encourage her to express her feelings, even if it's just a small amount. You should let her decide how fast to communicate and know you'll listen without judging. Knowing she can say what she wants is sometimes all it takes to help her work through her feelings.

Every week, a family I know sets aside time to "talk" or share anything on their minds. This helped their daughter feel more comfortable discussing her feelings about friends and first crushes. Over time, these talks changed on their own, giving her a regular, safe place to talk about how her feelings changed. These regular check-ins allowed her parents to support her as she worked through her feelings. This showed her that her feelings were of importance.

One psychologist, Carl Rogers, said, "It's a strange paradox that when I accept myself just as I am, I can grow." Making a safe place for honest talks helps people accept themselves. Knowing that she has the help to figure things out on her own terms gives her the courage to look at who she is.

We explore gender identity and expression without restrictions.

Identity and gender expression are essential parts of who we are, and giving someone a safe place to talk about them can be very powerful. It can be challenging to get to know yourself. She learns that her identity is valid and deserves respect when she feels empowered to ask questions and express her desires.

Start by giving them a simple, open-ended way to think about gender. Tell them that gender means different things to different people, and everyone has their own way of showing it. Tell her to think about what makes her feel comfortable, whether it's her clothes, her hobbies, or the way she feels inside. You shouldn't expect her to look or act certain. Let her find out what comes naturally, and reassure her that self-expression is about being true to yourself, not trying to fit in.

A mother I worked with had a daughter who loved to try on new clothes and sometimes picked out styles that didn't fit her gender. Her mother didn't push her toward more "feminine" styles; instead, she told her to experiment with different things and praised her imagination. This supported her daughter that she could explore creative ideas without fear of judgment. This helped her feel positive about her expression.

Don't forget to keep the discussion lively and open. Tell her she doesn't need to know everything about you. Identity is something we often find and change over time. "I am thankful to be a woman," Maya Angelou said. I must have accomplished something outstanding in a previous life, Maya Angelou said. This is a normal part of life. Encouragering her to keep exploring her uniqueness shows her that her identity is something to be proud of, not judged.

We provide guidance on romantic relationships appropriate for their age.

Learning how to be in a relationship can be exciting and difficult. By giving her advice that is right for her age, you're helping her deal with these feelings in a way that shows you understand and respect her. Talking about love doesn't mean forcing her to do things she's not ready for. It means helping her understand how she feels, see what a positive relationship looks like, and set limits that work for her.

Talk about what friendship and respect look like at the start, since they are the building blocks of any relationship. Tell them that trust, kindness, and respect for each other are the building blocks of a beneficial partnership. You should let her know that crushes are normal and part of growing up. She will understand that relationships should make her feel safe and valued if you talk about them in terms of friendship and respect.

One family I worked with talked about connections with their daughter through pictures and stories. When they watched a show with a love theme, they discussed the choices the characters made. They would also talk about what they thought was appropriate and inappropriate. This way of thinking helped her understand love in a straightforward manner. By talking about made-up cases, they helped her grasp real-life relationships without giving her too many complicated facts.

Let her know she can handle relationships and that no one should make her do anything she doesn't want. Her focus on freedom and respect teaches her to respect her limits. Some of the most respected therapists in the world say, "The quality of our relationships determines the quality of our lives." Teaching her this early on will enable her have healthy, satisfying relationships in the future.

<u>Change and Introspection</u>

By providing a safe space for her to discuss gender without fear of judgment and offering age-appropriate dating advice, you help her understand and accept her changing identity. Think about how these methods might help her: what small steps can lead to an open conversation about how she feels? How can you show her that who she is is real, no matter how it changes? And what kinds of models can help people understand love and respect?

Now that you have these insights, let's explore "What to Do About Peer Pressure."

How to Help Her Do It on Her Own

Being aware of your surroundings is a necessary skill for independence, but it can be challenging to teach generally. Role-playing makes this skill real and simple to use, and it gives her a chance to practice noticing her surroundings and acting in different situations. By assuming various roles, you provide her with a secure environment to experiment with various scenarios. You enhance her self-esteem, and teach her how to remain vigilant without succumbing to stress.

Start by thinking of simple things she might do every day. For example, crossing a busy street, traveling through a crowded area, or figuring out if someone is following her in a store. Start each scenario by telling her about the place and asking her to name anything interesting or important she saw. As an example, when she needs to cross the street, tell her to look for things like traffic lights, parked cars, and other people walking. She can practice responding by waiting for the light to change, looking both ways, or asking for help if she's unsure of what to do. Each situation shows her that being aware of what's going on around her makes her make smart choices.

One mother I know helped her daughter learn how to be situationally aware by acting out different social situations. For example, what to do if a stranger asks for help finding something? They would exchange roles and discuss appropriate responses, such as directing the individual to speak with a staff member. In addition, they would advise her not to approach strangers. These practice sessions helped her daughter learn how to handle unexpected events gently, which prepared her to handle them alone in real life.

Tell her to use this knowledge in real life, like keeping track of exits in an unfamiliar place. She can also notice sites on the way to a friend's house The famous explorer Bear Grylls sums up survival in three words: never give up. Situational awareness means teaching her to notice, evaluate, and trust her ability to safely manage her surroundings. This will give her the tools to be independent without fear.

Finding safe adults and reliable places to get help is crucial.

Knowing who to talk to when you don't know what to do helps. Teaching her how to find trusted people and places gives her a sense of safety and lets her know she has help when she needs it. By letting her know about safe people and places, you're showing her that being independent doesn't mean being alone; it means knowing where to get help when she needs it.

First, talk about the kinds of people who can help, like teachers, store workers, police officers, or neighbors. Make it clear that safe adults are people who are in charge or who have a specific job to do, like a library or crossing guard. Talk about times when she might need help, like if she gets lost, gets split from you in a public place, or feels uneasy around someone she doesn't know. You can tell these people are safe because they wear outfits or name tags. Remind her that it's okay to ask for help.

A family I worked with and their daughter made a map of "safe places." They marked on a map places in their neighborhood where she could go for help, like a neighbor's house, the library, or a store close by. They visited these places, said hello to the locals, and discussed how to help her. She felt safer and more independent when she knew she had a network of places and people she could trust. She felt like she could confidently get around her neighborhood.

Remind them that asking for help is not a sign of failing but of making a beneficial choice. This lesson teaches her that being independent means knowing when to ask for help. Maya Angelou once said, "Alone, all alone; nobody, but nobody, can make it out here alone." By helping her build a network of people and places she can trust, you teach her that being strong means knowing when and how to ask for help.

Giving clear examples to explain the difference between safe and dangerous behavior

She must understand the distinction between safe and dangerous behavior in order to become independent. Giving her clear examples helps her figure out how to evaluate situations, spot possible red flags, and decide when to back off or ask for help. Giving her specific, real-life examples helps her figure out what feels right and what doesn't, giving her the power to make choices based on her knowledge and gut feelings.

Explain that safe actions are those that respect her comfort, space, and limits. As an example, a teacher giving a high-five or a friend asking before taking something from her would be safe. On the other hand, someone asking her to keep a secret from her parents or trying to lead her somewhere alone could be dangerous. Giving her specific examples helps her figure out what to do instead of general directions like "trust your gut."

A family I knew taught their daughter about safety by acting out different situations, like what to do if an adult asks her to get in the car or if a stranger comes up to her on the field. They discussed clear actions she could take, such as saying "No, thank you," approaching a trusted adult, or calling a parent. Her daughter learned how to spot and deal with dangerous situations by seeing these examples. This gave her the confidence to say no and set limits.

Remind her that no one has the right to make her feel dangerous or nervous and tell her to speak up if she feels that way. Make it clear to her that she can leave a setting that doesn't feel right, whether that means turning down a small request or leaving a bigger commitment. Scientist Dr. Henry Cloud, who is known for his work on limits, has said, "Boundaries make us who we are." Teaching her these limits gives her the tools to keep herself safe and confident in her freedom.

<u>Change and Introspection</u>

You're giving her important skills for independence by teaching her to be aware of her surroundings. You're teaching her to find trusted people and trusted places, and tell the difference between safe and unsafe behaviors. Think about how these techniques can help her: what situations could benefit from role-playing? How can she practice finding places and people she trusts? What clear examples of limits can help her tell the difference between safe settings and unsafe settings?

So now that you have these basic skills, let's look at "Explaining Consent and Boundaries Clearly."

Making It Easy to Understand Consent and Limits

Your daughter will better understand agreement after learning about personal space and physical limits. Understanding personal space and its importance empowers her to establish her own boundaries and respect others'. Explain that personal space is everyone's "bubble" in simple terms. Some people prefer to stand close to others, while others prefer to be farther away.

You can start by using these ideas around the house. It can be enjoyable to alternately move closer and farther apart while asking each other, "Is this okay?" Or, "Is this too close?" This simple game teaches her that everyone is different when it comes to comfort and that it's okay and polite to check in with others. Remind her that she decides who can touch her and that she is free to say something if something makes her feel uncomfortable.

A family I knew piqued their daughter's interest in this concept by creating a game known as "bubble zone." They marked each family member's "bubble" with tape. They practiced asking each other for permission before entering into each other's space. This fun game helped their daughter understand personal space in a normal way. It made limits real and enjoyable.

Help her understand that different people have different privacy needs. For instance, she might be okay with hugging a close friend but prefer a high-five. "Daring to set boundaries is about having the courage to love ourselves, even when we risk disappointing others," said Dr. Brené Brown, a researcher known for her work on vulnerability and boundaries. Teaching her this early on can make her feel like her comfort matters and she controls her space.

Your girl can gain a powerful skill by saying "no" with confidence. It's not rude to tell her "no." It's about accepting her right to choose what's okay with her and knowing her boundaries. Teaching her to use "no" as a powerful yet gentle statement affirms her autonomy and respecting her limits.

Start by enacting various scenarios in which she might have to refuse "no." For instance, a friend might ask her to take something serious, or someone might ask her to do something she doesn't want to do. Tell her to say "no" in a cool, clear voice and look the other person in the eyes if it makes her feel better. Keep telling her that she doesn't have to say too much; a simple "No, thank you" or "I'd rather not" will do. She learns that "no" is an acceptable response by practicing this skill, which also makes it easier for her to stand up for herself without feeling negative about it.

There was a mom I knew who helped her daughter learn how to refuse "no" by giving her choices. They would practice saying "no" to things like sharing a favorite toy or politely turning down an offer. For her daughter, this helped her understand that saying "no" didn't mean she was mean; it meant she respected her comfort level. She learned over and over again that it was okay to set limits, even with people she liked and trusted.

Oprah Winfrey often said, "You only have to accept yes to the things that bring you joy." Knowing she can respond "no" when necessary enhances her self-esteem. Teaching her that saying "no" is beneficial and not detrimental gives her the courage to stand up for herself in a way that is polite and feels normal.

Her personal experience shows her that consent is more than permission—it's about respect. Asking for and giving permission easily and without pressure is consent. Once she knows this, she can easily give or refuse consent in any situation. This will help her feel more in control of her body and comfort.

Start by providing her with examples she already knows. Say something like, "Let's assume you want to borrow a friend's book." You would ask first, right? You would accept her choice if she said "no." This straightforward example demonstrates the exchange of consent and the unquestionable respect for "no" as a complete response. Make it clear that everyone can say "no," and respecting others' limits is as significant as her own.

Talk about school or social events, too. For instance, if someone asks for a hug, tell her that it's okay to respond with "No, that's not okay with me" or give something else, like a high-five. Teaching her this concept helps her feel in charge while learning how to be kind and clear in social situations. Talking about different events helps her remember that permission is a general rule she can use all her life.

In their home, a family I knew always sought permission before hugging or touching someone's belongings. This showed their daughter that asking permission is critical, even for close family members. Over time, she got better at asking for permission herself, which made the family a place where everyone felt valued.

"Boundaries are the distance at which I can love you and me simultaneously," said Dr. Gabor Maté, a specialist in trauma and childhood development. Teaching her to set and respect boundaries through real-life situations gives her a balanced and respectful understanding of consent that she can apply to all of her relationships.

<u>Change and Introspection</u>

You're teaching her to respect herself and others by giving her personal space, teaching her how to say "no," and letting her practice real-life consent situations. Think about how these skills can help her: what models can help her understand personal space? How could role-playing help her feel more comfortable saying "no"? What examples from real life show how significant permission is?

Now that you have acquired these crucial skills for respect and freedom, let's discuss "Talking About Romance, Gender, and Identity" together.

WE DISCUSS LOVE, GENDER, AND AUTHENTICITY.

Setting up a safe place where people can talk freely about their feelings

Knowing how you feel about love, gender, and identity is difficult. Making her feel supported by giving her a safe place to talk about her feelings is the first step. When she understands that she can speak to you about anything, she learns that her feelings are okay, even if they seem strange or challenging to understand. She feels safe knowing you're honest and doesn't have to face this alone.

Start by being open with her when talking to her. Tell her that it's normal to experience any way she does, whether it's anxious, confused, or uncertain. Don't give advice or draw conclusions immediately. Instead, listen to her and encourage her to express her feelings, even if it's just a small amount. You should let her decide how fast to talk and let her know that you'll listen without judging. Knowing she can say what she wants is sometimes all it takes to help her work through her feelings.

Every week, a family I know sets aside time to "talk" or share anything on their minds without interruptions. This helped their daughter feel more comfortable discussing her feelings about friends and first crushes. Over time, these talks changed on their own, giving her a regular, safe place to talk about how her feelings were changing. These regular check-ins allowed her parents to support her as she worked through her feelings. This showed her that her feelings were important.

One psychologist, Carl Rogers, said, "It's a strange paradox that when I accept myself just as I am, then I can change." Making a safe place for honest talks helps people accept themselves. Knowing that she has the help to figure things out on her own terms gives her the courage to look into who she is.

Identity and gender expression are essential parts of who we are, and giving someone a safe place to talk about them can be very powerful. It can be challenging to get to know yourself. She learns that her identity is valid and deserves respect when she feels empowered to ask questions and express her desires.

Start by giving them a simple, open-ended way to think about gender. Tell them that gender means different things to different people, and everyone has their own way of showing it. Tell her to think about what makes her feel happy, whether it's her clothes, her hobbies, or the way she feels inside. You shouldn't expect her to look or act certain. Let her find out what comes naturally, and reassure her that self-expression is about being true to yourself, not trying to fit in.

A mother I worked with had a daughter who loved to try new clothes and sometimes picked out styles that didn't fit her gender. Her mother didn't push her toward more "feminine" styles; instead, she told her to try different things and praised her imagination. This support demonstrated to her daughter that she could explore new ideas without fear of judgment. This helped her feel positive about how she expressed herself.

Don't forget to keep the discussion going and open. Tell her she doesn't need to know everything about you. Identity is something we often find and change over time. "I am thankful to be a woman," Maya Angelou said. I must have accomplished something outstanding in a previous life, Maya Angelou said. This is a normal part of life, and encouraging her to keep exploring her uniqueness shows her that her identity is something to be proud of, not judged.

Learning how to be in a relationship can be exciting and difficult. By giving her advice that is right for her age, you're helping her deal with these feelings in a way that shows you understand and respect her. Talking about love doesn't mean forcing her to do things she's not ready for. It means helping her understand how she feels, see what a positive relationship looks like, and set limits that work for her.

Talk about what friendship and respect look like at the start, since they are the building blocks of any relationship. Tell them that trust, kindness, and respect for each other are the building blocks of a beneficial partnership. You should let her know that crushes are normal and part of growing up. She will understand that relationships should make her feel safe and valued if you talk about them in terms of friendship and respect.

One family I worked with talked about connections with their daughter through pictures and stories. When they watched a show with a love theme, they would talk about the choices the characters made. They would also talk about what they thought was appropriate and inappropriate. This way of thinking helped her understand love in a straightforward way. By talking about made-up cases, they helped her comprehend real-life relationships without giving her too many complicated facts.

Let her know she can handle relationships and that no one should make her do anything she doesn't want. Her focus on freedom and respect teaches her to respect her limits. Some of the most qualified therapists in the world say, "The quality of our relationships determines the quality of our lives." Teaching her this early on will help her have healthy, satisfying relationships in the future.

<u>Change and Introspection</u>

By providing a safe space for her to discuss gender without fear of judgment and offering age-appropriate dating advice, you help her understand and accept her changing identity. Think about how these methods might help her: what small steps can lead to an open conversation about how she feels? How can you show her that who she is is real, no matter how it changes? And what kinds of models can help people understand love and respect?

Now that you have these insights, let's explore "What to Do About Peer Pressure."

CONCLUSION

"It is not our differences that divide us. It is our inability to recognize, accept, and celebrate those differences." – Audre Lorde

Building your daughter's self-esteem, independence, and happiness along her path is critical.

As you've read this guide, each part gives you a plan for how to help, empower, and praise your daughter. Let's go over the main ideas again and add to them. We should also consider how each component contributes to her growth in self-assurance, independence, and happiness.

<u>Chapter 1: What You Need to Know About Autism in Girls</u>

The first thing we did on our trip was learn about how autism shows up differently in girls. Understanding the various manifestations of your daughter's autism enabled us to decipher her potential misinterpretation or delayed diagnosis. You learned more about her world by lookingato how gender roles, hormone differences, and social training affect her life. This chapter made you think about autism not as a problem but as a part of her uniquepersonality. Thist shapes her strengths, views, and even problems.

This chapter expanded on these concepts, emphasizing that comprehending her inner world is the initial step towards understanding and caring for her. Understanding her will enable you to advocate for her, enhance her self-esteem, and foster acceptance of her. Knowing her unique way of seeing the world makes your relationship with her stronger and gives her self-respect.

<u>Chapter 2: Dealing with feelings and sensory issues</u>

We discussed practical strategies to manage intense emotions and sensory challenges. This section provided her with tools to find peace amidst life's challenges. These tools included strategies for managing anxiety and rejection sensitivity, as well as techniques for creating a peaceful environment. In each part, she learned how to identify emotional triggers, create personalized anxiety toolkits, and practice mindfulness. This helped her maintain her composure in a stressful world.

The chapter delved into more detail about these techniques. It stressed how critical it is to make her feel safe exploring and expressing her feelings in a caring and accepting environment. You're giving her tools for life that will help her be strong and stable by showing her how to handle her inner world. Taking care of her emotions isn't just a way for her to deal with things; it's a base for her mental health that helps her grow with a strong sense of inner peace.

Chapter 3: Autism as a child

As she gets older, she faces new challenges, such as puberty and her body image. She also learns how to make friends and get along with others. This section provided her with age-appropriate strategies for discussing changes in her body, fostering a positive self-image, and teaching her how to connect with others. It gave her ways to make friends based on mutual respect and hobbies. It also gave her ways to learn social interaction rules, which can be challenging to understand at times.

By adding to this advice, we stress that every step of growth is a chance to learn more about oneself. You're helping her become a strong young woman who knows and respects her body. She values her uniqueness, and feels free to make deep connections by being there for her as she moves through challenging changes. She has an unusual road to follow as she grows up with autism. By spending time with her, you give her the support she needs to face these changes with pride and confidence.

Chapter 4: Learning and Talking to People

This section discussed strategies for finding her voice, whether through verbal or nonverbal communication, and advocating for her educational needs. Connections between lessons and her special hobbies and encouraging her self-expression in different ways made school more approachable. Communication isn't just about letting her say what she wants; it's also about making her feel heard and giving her a chance to speak up for herself.

To build on these ideas, we discussed how helping her way of learning and communicating boosts her confidence in and out of the classroom. Upon witnessing the fulfillment of her needs, she recognizes her entitlement to attention and assistance. You're not only helping her do better at school, but also teaching her how to speak up for herself. This is a valuable skill that makes her feel more independent and positive about her own worth.

<u>Chapter 5: Being safe, sexual, and making friends</u>

As she becomes more independent, it's a necessity for her to understand limits, agreements, and her own safety. This part told you how to teach her about safe relationships, help her figure out who she is, and set limits. Each part stressed how critical it was to use clear, polite language to help her deal with relationships and her own safety. This gave her the freedom to make decisions based on her values.

By adding to these lessons, you're showing her that her freedom and limits are significant. She learns that people should listen to her, comfort her, and care about her feelings. This boosts her confidence and helps her stand up for herself in social situations. With these tools, she feels more confident in her ability to build supportive and polite partnerships while still having self-respect.

Every chapter builds on the one before it, giving her a complete plan for growth, confidence, and freedom. Knowing how her autism affects her in such a profound way, teaching her critical life skills, and building a community of support gives her a sense of self-worth and strength that will last her whole life.

Think about how you can keep building her skills. What tools can she use to feel positive about each new step? And how can you continue to create an environment where love, respect, and happiness are commonplace?

Supporting her doesn't just mean helping her get through challenging times; it also means praising her for who she is, telling her to be proud of her journey, and giving her the strength to face the world with bravery and self-respect. Thanks for putting in so much effort to support her grow. You are her biggest fan, and supporting her on her unique path with love and care.

By following these rules, you're helping her grow into a happy, confident young woman who is ready to enjoy everything life has to offer.

RESOURCES

https://autisticgirlsnetwork.org/

https://www.autismempowerment.org/resource-center/resources-for-females-on-the-autism-spectrum/

https://www.autismspeaks.org/finding-your-community

https://aane.org/services-programs/group-services/support-groups-community-connection

https://www.neurodiversityweek.com/events

https://www.meetup.com/audhd-online-community/

https://autism.org/neurodiversity-celebration-week/

https://nationalautismassociation.org/family-support/find-a-support-group/

https://www.autismempowerment.org/resource-center/resources-for-females-on-the-autism-spectrum/support-organizations/

As a way of saying thanks for your purchase, I'm offering the book Shadow Work Journal: A Journey of Self-Discovery for FREE to my readers.

To get instant access just go to:

Inside the book, you will discover:

- How to uncover hidden aspects of yourself through guided prompts

- Techniques for integrating your shadow self into your conscious life

- Exercises to foster emotional growth and self-awareness

- Practical tips for creating a balanced and fulfilling life

If you want to embark on a journey of self-discovery and transformation, make sure to grab the free book.